Roger Mortimer was born in 1909 and was educated at Eton and Sandhurst. In 1930 he was commissioned into the Coldstream Guards. He fought at Dunkirk in 1940 and was taken as a POW for the remainder of the war. After resigning from the army in 1947, he became a racing correspondent for the *Sunday Times* for almost thirty years. He wrote several classic books on racing including *The History of the Derby*. He met Cynthia Denison-Pender in 1947 and was married the same year. They had two daughters: Jane and Louise and one son, Charles. Roger died in 1991.

Louise Mortimer was educated at Yateley Hall, Daneshill and Tudor Hall. She has had a mixed career history: PR to an antiques dealer, sales assistant, professional cook, kindergarten teacher at Garden House School, volunteer teacher for various charities in India and Mauritius. She has two children, Rebecca and Benjamin, and is currently semi-retired and living peacefully with slightly overweight border terrier, Marley Mortimer, in London.

DEAR LUMPY...

Roger Mortimer and Louise Mortimer

Constable • London

Constable & Robinson Ltd
55–56 Russell Square
London WC1B 4HP
www.constablerobinson.com

First published in the UK by Constable,
an imprint of Constable & Robinson, 2013

Published in this paperback edition by Constable, 2014

A copy of the British Library Cataloguing in
Publication data is available from the British Library

ISBN 978-1-47211-126-5 (hardback)
ISBN 978-1-47210-928-6 (ebook)

1 3 5 7 9 10 8 6 4 2

Printed and bound in the UK

For Rebecca and Benjamin

An Introduction from my Brother Lupin

My delightful younger sister gave me the great honour of choosing the cover photograph for her book, *Dear Lumpy* . . .

'But you can't see my face!' was her immediate response. 'Precisely!' was mine.

In 2011, I got together with publishers Constable & Robinson to produce a small book as a tribute to my long suffering parents. *Dear Lupin* . . . was based around letters sent to me from my father and it would not be an exaggeration to say that expectations for sales were not that high. My father, although well known in racing circles, had been dead for over twenty years and I had barely read a book let alone compiled one before. At the first meeting with my editor he made the situation very clear: 'You're quite funny but nowhere near as funny as your father so I would be most grateful if you would keep your literary contribution in this book to a bare minimum.'

Originally *Dear Lupin* . . . was going to be printed in a run of 3,500 copies and even then I had visions of trying to flog unsold books together with pots of homemade chutney at local Conservative Party bazaars. The publishers didn't exactly boost my confidence when they asked me at one stage how many friends did I have. However, as luck would have it, *Dear Lupin . . .* sold rather better than anticipated and to my utter astonishment ended up as BBC Radio 4 'Book of the Week'.

Throughout all this I was fully supported not only by 'my other half' but also by my younger sister known in the family as Lumpy (or when in an uncommunicative mood as the 'Lump with the Hump'). It was only recently, however, having always led us to believe she only had kept about ten letters to her from our father, that she finally came clean to the fact that she had a couple of hundred. Thus with a bit of arm-twisting I dragged her along to my legendary agent Maggie Hanbury and *Dear Lumpy . . .* was born. The letters to my sister, who was twelve years old at the time of the early ones, are a lot of fun and my dad clearly enjoys mobbing her and her friends up (as indeed do I). The letters are of a very different tone to the ones I received, which were largely of concern and exasperation, but equally witty and affectionate.

When *Dear Lupin . . .* was published I made it very clear (to anybody who could be bothered to listen) that my dad had done all the writing and the humour. I merely contributed twenty-five years of disorderly conduct. Thus I felt a complete fraud when introduced as an author and felt that describing myself as one took disingenuous to boundaries not even tested by Tony Blair. This seemed to amuse Lumpy and her son Benjamin considerably (for some bizarre reason) and they made threats to give me a T-shirt with 'I am NOT an author' printed on it. So I am delighted she finds herself in an identical situation.

I wish her and my father every success with *Dear Lumpy . . .*

Charlie Mortimer

Preface

Even after the surprise success of my brother's tribute to our father, *Dear Lupin . . .*, I made it clear, to anyone who was remotely interested, that I had absolutely no intention of producing a similar book myself. This was despite being endlessly asked: 'Have you kept the letters from your father?' or 'Are the letters he sent you as funny and touching as the letters he wrote to your brother?' However, rather surprisingly, it was my brother who persuaded me to actually dig out all the letters I had and read them.

I thought I had close to fifty cards and letters. As it turned out there were nearer two hundred. I read several of these to close friends who laughed until they had tears running down their cheeks. Then, with much encouragement and assistance from my brother, I started putting together this second tribute book to my father. We have not forgotten, of course, the inimitable character that was our dear mother who always had our best interests at heart and never failed to give us unusual advice and make rather extraordinary observations – such as on the way home from my father's sister's funeral when she remarked: 'Do you know what? I think that's the most fun we've ever had with Aunt Joan.'

The whole process of reading and sorting my father's letters has been a challenge as I had not read any of them since his death in 1991, and not one letter had a date on it which included the year and I had not kept the envelopes. It was all extremely emotional and I found myself laughing, crying, and sometimes even laughing and crying at the same time. Above all, though, this magical inheritance, which had been kept in a drawer for over twenty years, brought my father and indeed my entire family back to life in a way that I would never have thought possible.

To say that I am proud of my father is an understatement. Growing up I was a 'daddy's girl' and in my eyes he could do no wrong. Being the youngest and a daughter, my father was much more lenient and I was impossibly spoilt as I could twist him around my little finger. Having said that, he was like a rock and in times of need he was always there for me – wise, kind and always calm. I don't remember him ever losing his temper. If he was annoyed, angry or upset about a situation he would just take to his typewriter and we would receive a dressing down that also managed to be loving – a real skill. I am eternally grateful to both my parents for not giving up on me despite their disappointment when I was excluded from one of the country's premier girls' schools for misconduct and for marrying my much disapproved of boyfriend, Henry, in secret.

Dear Lumpy . . . is a companion volume to *Dear Lupin . . .* and the letters in the book are a further snapshot of all the ups and downs, the trials and tribulations of life with the Mortimers and their friends.

A Bit of History

My dad was born Roger Francis Mortimer on 22 November 1909. My grandparents were pretty well off and lived in a house in Cadogan Gardens, Chelsea, London. According to the 1911 census there were eight 'live-in' staff members. My grandfather, Haliburton Stanley Mortimer, was a charming man but by all accounts not a great stockbroker. My grandmother, Dorothy (née Blackwell) was an heiress of the well-known food company Crosse & Blackwell. My father had one sibling, Joan, born in 1907.

He was educated at Ludgrove School, Eton College and Sandhurst. In 1930 he was commissioned into the Coldstream Guards. He was a captain when his platoon fought a desperate rear guard action at Dunkirk in 1940 during which almost all of his men were killed and he was wounded. Unconscious, he was taken prisoner and spent the remainder of the war in prison camps running the camp radio. Many of my father's friends in later life were those he met as prisoner-of-war no. 481 in various Oflags and Stalags.

After the war he rejoined his regiment and, as a major, served in Trieste. However, in 1947 he resigned and took up an appointment with Raceform, the official form book for horse racing. He followed this by becoming racing correspondent of the *Sunday Times* until retiring almost thirty years later. He also wrote for various other newspapers, was a commentator for the BBC and became PR officer to the Tote. In addition, he wrote several classic books on racing, the greatest of which was undoubtedly *The History of the Derby*. His other books on racing included *The Jockey Club, Anthony Mildmay, Twenty Great Horses* and *The Flat*. My dad was also a keen gardener and quite an expert on military history.

He met my mother, Cynthia Denison-Pender, in 1947 and within six weeks had proposed to her. They were married in St Paul's, Knightsbridge, on 10 December of the same year. My older sister Jane was born in 1949, my brother Charlie in 1952 and myself in 1957.

Dramatis Personae

Family

My ex-husband: Henry Carew aka Hot Hand Henry, HHH (married 1977; divorced).

My children: Rebecca Cunningham aka Beckie (née Carew, born 20 September 1978, married Darren Cunningham, 2009); Benjamin Carew aka Ben (born 25 July 1985).

My mother: Cynthia Sydney Mortimer aka Nidnod (née Denison-Pender, born 28 February 1921).

My older sister: Jane Clare Torday aka Miss Bossy Pants (née Mortimer, born 23 January 1949).

My brother: Charlie Mortimer aka Lupin (born 4 April 1952).

My brother's civil partner: Tim Partington.

My brothers-in-law: Paul Torday (married Jane, 1971; two sons, Piers and Nick; divorced); Tommy Bates (married Jane, 2003).

Father's mother: Dorothy Mortimer aka Gar (née Blackwell).

Father's sister: Joan Cockburn (née Mortimer, born 1907; married to Reggie Cockburn aka Uncle Reggie).

Mother's sisters: Pamela Darling aka Aunt Pam, The Hamburger (née Denison-Pender, born 1915; married to Kenneth Darling aka Uncle Ken, Uncle Whiskers); Barbara Fellowes aka Aunt Boo (née Denison-Pender, born 1917; divorced).

Father's first cousins: Tom Blackwell; John Blackwell.

Father's first cousins once removed: Tom Blackwell's son, Charlie, and daughter, Caroline.

Father's aunts: Shirley Blackwell (née Lawson-Johnson); Margery Blackwell (never married).

Mother's aunt: Phyllis Shedden aka Aunt Pips (née Fisher; married Norman Loder, then Lindsay Shedden).

Family pets

Turpin (black mongrel); Moppet (the cat); Pongo (Dalmatian); Soloman Grundy aka Tiny Man, Solly, Cringer (fox terrier); Peregrine aka Perry (Chihuahua); Baron von Otto aka The Baron, Otto (Chihuahua); Jester (horse); Golly (horse); Danny (Chihuahua).

My pets

Chappie (Yorkshire terrier); Kimber (big black mongrel); Leo (horse).

Gardeners

Mr Randall aka Randy; Keith Bailey.

Domestics

Mabel (my father's nanny); Jenny; Audrey; Joy; Dawn.

Neighbours

Colin and Sarah Bomer (also close family friends), and their two sons, Mark and William; the Roper-Caldbecks; Farmer Luckes; Lord Carnarvon; Serena and Bob Alexander and their two boys.

Dad's prisoner-of-war friends

John Surtees aka Mr S. (and wife Anne); Desmond Parkinson aka Mr P. (and wives Heather, then Paddy); Freddy Burnaby-Atkins (and wife Jenny); Fitz Fletcher; Francis Reed; Sir Frederick Corfield QC aka Dungy Fred.

Dad's horse-racing friends

Nick and Judy Gaselee; John (my godfather) and Liz Pope; Peter Willett and his two sons, Stephen and David; John and Jean Hislop; the Cottrills; Dick Hern; Peter Walwyn; the Wallis family; Cecil Langton-May (my godfather); Dick Francis; Willie Carson; John Abergavenny; Gordon Richards; Lester Piggott; Brough Scott.

Other family friends

Lord Belper aka Ronnie Belper; the Camerons (Agnete Cameron – my mother's best friend); Gerald and Helen de Mauley aka Lady de Mauley (my godmother); Rodney Carrott; Raoul, Sheelagh and Emma Lemprière-Robin; the Grissells; the Tollers; the Thistlethwaytes; the Edgedales; the Blackers; the Hambros; Lady Rumbold aka Nika the

Squeaker; Lady Camilla Pender (my godmother); Helen and Bobby Kennard.

My headmistresses

Miss Vallence (Headmistress at Daneshill); Mrs Blythe (Headmistress at Tudor Hall).

My friends

Charlotte Duthie (née Blacker); Xandra Makim (née Cameron); Kate Lluberes (née Evans); Emma Belak (née Edgedale); Andy Loch; Diana Clapham aka Tiny; Julian Seaman.

Other characters and acquaintances

Lady Kennard and Sir George Kennard aka Loopy (my in-laws); Mrs Carew (HHH's grandmother); the Guinnesses; the Lloyd Webbers.

Lupin's friends

Charlie Hurt; Robin Grant-Sturgis; Molly Salisbury aka the Marchioness of Salisbury; George Rodney; Charlie Shearer; Patrick Fisher; James Staples; Pete Breitmeyer aka Peter Carew; Jeremy Soames; Joe Gibbs; the Hobbs brothers.

Family homes

Barclay House, Yateley (1950–67); Budds Farm, Burghclere (1967–84); The Miller's House, Kintbury (1984–2006).

On 12 January 1957 I arrived in the world. My father had been at the Newbury race meeting, commentating on the radio. My mother wrote in my pink 'baby book': 'Louise Star Mortimer, like Charles, was born at Barclay House. The day was spent getting any last minute things ready. I took to my bed at 4 p.m. and Louise arrived at 8.27 p.m. She was wonderfully round and pink faced with a shock of dark hair. Roger came upstairs immediately to have a look at her. After announcing that he thought she looked as though she had character, he took Dr Hadfield (our family doctor and friend) downstairs for a drink.'

Moving on twelve years I have just started at a weekly boarding school . . .

1969

The Flappings
Much Nattering
Berkshire

My Dearest Lumpy,

I hope you are settling down well and have not been moistening your pillow with hot tears. Settle down to some steady work and kindly refrain from doing anything really foolish. I miss you very much here and so does Cringer. Have you had a letter from the man with the Rolls Royce yet?

You have now got to the age when most girls have clashes of policy and opinion with their mothers. I shall be surprised if you prove an exception. My advice to you is to play it dead cool and decline to be drawn into long and acrimonious arguments. Your mother is devoted to your interests but like other mothers she is not always reasonable; nor, of course, are you.

I greatly enjoy having you at home but think there are grounds for improvement in your manners with people (not your parents) older than yourself. Your attitude sometimes borders on the oafish and if visitors make the effort to be agreeable to you, you must reciprocate. At times you seem to make no effort at all; possibly from shyness, more probably from sheer laziness and a disinclination to exert your mind at all. I shall anticipate marked improvement next holidays!

How is Snouter? I trust you will look after him during the winter. One of our big trees has got elm disease and has got to be cut down. Your sister Jane has been attacked by fleas and mosquitoes in Greece. The new people came into the cottage on Saturday. Pongo has sore feet and is very smelly.

Best love,

D

Snouter was a gingham toy pig bought from a local fete. My father gives some practical advice regarding my mother; being a typical teenager, it goes straight in one ear and out the other.

The Sunday Times

Dearest Lumpy,

If you ever leave bits of stick and bamboo all over the lawn again, thereby mucking up the mowing machine, I will string you up to the laundry line and flog you for 2½ hours with long boughs of freshly cut holly. So watch it and don't push your luck too far! I enclose some sweepstake tickets. You may win a pink plastic po or a bottle of home-made wine derived from parsnips and old cabbage stalks. Jane is in a great dither and talks at interminable length on the telephone. It is so tiring for those who have to listen. Pongo has caught a small rat and Cringer, I fear, has worms. I hope to see you again soon. Don't eat too many sweets or you will burst out of all your new clothes.

Best love,

D

I have annoyed my father again. He deals with it this time by using idle threats. I am persona non grata.

Budds Farm
23 November

Dear Miss Plumpling,

Thank you so much for remembering my birthday and sending me both a most acceptable present and an exceptionally pert card. It is v. cold here and I simply cannot afford to turn the heating on yet. I go to bed in long woollen socks and a balaclava helmet which lets the cold air in owning [*sic*] to the depredations by hostile moths. Your mother is in bed with a sore throat caused, in my view, by talking too much without appropriate pauses for thought. She has announced her intention to go to Kenya after Christmas. Will you come here as cook? Or perhaps I will just get on a boat and go off somewhere. Possibly China. More likely the Isle of Wight. Cringer is in good form and has just eaten four petit beurre biscuits. No wonder he is getting thick round the neck. Your mother kindly gave me a shirt for my birthday. Alas, it would have fitted William Bomer.

    Best love,

    D

My father always pleaded poverty, especially when it came to heating the house or paying the phone bill. In very cold weather he would wear his balaclava and a very fetching jersey he had knitted out of old blanket wool when he was a prisoner-of-war.

1970

The Sunday Times
16 May

Dear Miss Mingy,

I am relieved to hear you have passed (by a very narrow margin) into Tudor Hall School for pert young ladies but doubt if I shall be able to pay the bills so you may not be there long. I hope you behaved well during your visit to the Blackers and did not pinch the spoons and were not sick on the drawing-room carpet. I always think Miss C. Blacker is very pretty and attractive. We had a nice visit to Colonel and Mrs Nickalls apart from getting lost on the way. Moppet has killed a large mole and Cringer has made a series of large pools – almost lakes – in the kitchen. I have heard nothing of Lupin but your sister jabbers away incessantly and does not seem to know whether it is Christmas or Easter. The Head Mistress at Tudor Hall is exceptionally strict and has the reputation of being the most relentless flogger in the business today. So just watch it and mind your manners! I enclose a small present. Don't just buy milk chocolate or you will soon have the same waistline as the oldest and greediest elephant at Billy Smart's Circus.

Best love,

D

At thirteen my whole class at Daneshill moved on to other schools. My parents chose Tudor Hall for me on the advice of my brother Lupin! Not exactly the world expert on premier girls' schools.

Budds Farm

Dear Louise,

You really are the limit. I opened my box of saccharine tablets this morning and there was a dead cockroach there. I think that was a joke on your part in quite exceptionally bad taste. This time, in fact, you have pushed your luck just a bit too far. I intend to stop your pocket money till 1975 and to engage a holiday governess, Miss Beatrice Birchenough, who has been working in a reform school for difficult girls and knows just how to deal with really hard cases. I may try a few reprisals myself, so don't be surprised if you find a very old cod's head neatly sewn up in your pillow one night. I have in the meantime written a stiff note to Miss Vallence suggesting that you and the members of your dormitory are completely out of hand and a dangerous threat to their ever-loving parents. The workmen have just finished doing the drive. They came in for a cup of tea and have left tar all over the kitchen floor. I fear your dear mother may explode when she discovers. I believe you are coming home for a long weekend. I challenge you to a croquet match for 5/. You are allowed a start of two up but just for once you must forbear from cheating. By the way, thanks awfully for your outstanding generosity in offering me one of those chocolates I bought for you. I found a huge toad in the woodshed today and intend to adopt him as he is very friendly and from a certain angle reminds me slightly of your plump sister Jane. I shall feed him on a diet of bread and milk and dead flies. Tomorrow I have to go to your Great-aunt Margery's funeral. She was 84 and had been like a hard-boiled egg for years.

Best of love and do try and keep out of trouble if you can otherwise I can see you ending up in Borstal rather than at Tudor Hall.

D xx

I get an enormous amount of pleasure from playing practical jokes on my family. I have been known to put fish heads in my sister's makeup bag and paint skulls in luminous paint on the walls of the spare room when my brother-in-law is staying.

Budds Farm
Sunday

My Dearest Louise,

I trust you are now well prepared for your confirmation

and have adjusted your plump face to a very holy expression. Please keep it like that till after the service, during which you are forbidden to suck sweets or chew gum. Will you be dressed in white, a colour signifying, rather absurdly in certain cases which I will not mention, innocence and purity? Do you have to wear a white hat, and will it be composed of hen feathers or half an old tablecloth? As I shall be the most pure and innocent person there, I propose to come in a white suit. However, enough of that. We must all be very solemn and listen with the closest attention to what the Bishop says; I am sure it will be very good for us. It is a very long time since I was confirmed at Eton. I put on a clean collar and a lot of Anzora Hair Cream (IT MASTERS THE HAIR, so it said on the bottle) which made my hair stiff like cardboard. It was most unfortunate that the Bishop quite forgot to turn up and we were in Chapel for nearly two hours before a substitute could be obtained. Luckily none of my god-parents were there, but my mother was. She was not a great church-goer and got very restive during the long wait. Fortunately I had brought a book in with me as over 100 boys were being confirmed and I knew it would be a very long service indeed even if everything went well.

However, to be more serious for a moment, I am sure it is all 'a good thing' and if you think hard about it just occasionally you may see the point of it all and derive some benefit. I'm sure your mother still does, and perhaps most of us do during times of stress and difficulty. However, one's religion is a very personal matter and it is all really up to you. I rather envy those who have a settled religious faith; it gives them a feeling of security.

I hope you realise it is a strict rule that no sweets are eaten for 17 days after confirmation and it is the custom to hand over all pocket money to the poor of the parish. To save you the trouble, I have already done that on your behalf. At least I would have done had there been any poor in the parish, but there are not. After the expenses of Jane's wedding, I reckon I am poorer than most so I am retaining the money for myself. I'm sure you will agree that this was the right and proper course.

That revolting Moppet left a rabbit's head under the dining room table; it was found by Pongo who made short work of it, to the great disgust of your mother. We are going to have quite a lot of strawberries and raspberries; what a pity they upset your stomach so and you are unable to eat them. I really feel sorry for you. However, I will see your mother makes you some nice junket or tapioca pudding instead.

Thank goodness we have a quiet day here today. I feel very exhausted. On Tuesday I leave at 5 a.m. and motor up to Newmarket. I come back early on Wednesday as I may have to go to a funeral at Rotherwick in the afternoon before I move on to you.

Your affectionate father,

RM

From an early age the relationship I have with my father is very affectionate. Although confirmation is a serious occasion I revel in being mobbed up by him and I am more likely to heed serious advice when accompanied by witty stories and leg pulling.

1971

Budds Farm
23 June

My Dear Lumpy,

I think that card from you and Sandra was amazingly cheeky and I intend to take steps when next we meet to extract a grovelling apology. So just watch it, you two. I will have you howling for mercy in a very short time indeed. I don't think Sandra will be able to run very fast in those very tight jeans she wears; also she eats so much that her speed has been greatly reduced. As for you, I warn you. I found a dead rat on the rubbish heap in the garden; it is now in your room and it is up to you to find it. The smell and the fleas may offer some valuable clues. I hope you are doing extremely well in your examinations. A man in Basingstoke kept his daughter in a damp cellar on bread and water for a month after she had failed in her O levels; that is nothing to what I shall do to you if you fail to get a brilliant report. Jenny has got hay fever and

Cringer has worms. The strawberries are rotting because of all the rain. Far too many people are coming to Jane's wedding and most of them I have never even heard of. I am barring men with beards and women with bare feet and dirty toenails. I hope you will not drink too much champagne as I don't want to see you rolling about on the carpet in your best suit. I am trying to get Lupin to wash his neck for the occasion.

Best love,

D

I am oblivious to the fraught lead up to my older sister Jane's wedding. Lupin left the Coldstream Guards just before being commissioned, which went down like a lead balloon across the family, especially with Uncle Whiskers (aka General Sir Kenneth Darling, commander-in-chief of Allied Forces Northern Europe).

Budds Farm

Dearest L,

I am sorry not to have heard from you since you went back. Perhaps though you wrote to Nidnod and she forgot to show me the letter. We set off to France on the 29th. The weather forecast was 'very stormy indeed' and the car ferries were running hours late. I did not much like the prospect as those old ferry boats roll hideously. We got to Dover and nearly got on the wrong boat by mistake. Eventually we drove on to a dreadful, creaking old boat; there was only one other car on it. We had a cabin, fell fast asleep and did not wake up till we arrived at Dunkirk at 4 a.m. We then had a long drive in appalling rainstorms to Chantilly, stopping for breakfast at a small service station where the food was far less nasty than at similar places in England. We arrived at Chantilly very weary at 8.30 a.m. and found to our horror that our hotel, usually empty at this time of the year, was full on account of May 1st being a Public Holiday. We were eventually given a room in a small inn where they were clearing up after an all-night wedding party. Your mother retired to bed (the sheets bore both hand and foot prints of previous occupants, while my pillow had clearly been used by a large and very hairy dog with dirty paws) with a hot water bottle. An hour later Nidnod woke up to find the bottle had leaked and the bed was soaking. She was certain that the hotel proprietor would think she had wetted her bed so we turned the mattress. What we found on the other side I simply cannot tell you. However we re-made the bed more or less successfully. In the meantime I had shaved but could not make the water disappear. Investigation revealed that the previous occupant had been sick in the basin and had blocked the drain! Thanks very much. We then set off for the races at Longchamp in warm, sunny weather. We got lost in Paris, Nidnod was almost in hysterics and I was terrified by the French drivers who have no manners at all. We got there in the end and met the Hislops, who gave us a wonderful and most expensive lunch in a superb restaurant on top of the grandstand. We saw Mill Reef win and then returned to Chantilly, Nidnod at the wheel. She nearly went broadside-on into a French car and death was very close indeed at that moment. She then got hopelessly lost trying to find the Ring Road and we drove for hours round Paris without making any headway. We were both exhausted by then and it would have been a relief if we had been mown down by a giant lorry. However we at last got back and had a very good dinner to cheer us up. The following morning I had to see some of the best horses in France at Chantilly, which I enjoyed, and we then drove some 170 miles to Deauville where we had a restful night in a comfortable hotel. The next day I had to visit a stud and then we had a marvellous lunch at a small restaurant at Bonneville-sur-Mer. Your mother ordered a king-size dish of lobsters, crabs, mussels, clams, prawns etc and I was not all that surprised when she had a bad attack of diarrhoea (not an easy word to spell) afterwards. We then drove to Clecy and were given a very warm welcome at the little hotel we go to there. The weather was perfect the next day and we went up on the hills which are covered with wild flowers of every sort. We had a superb lunch out of doors by the side of a river with your god-mother Diana Gunn and her boozy but affable husband. We did not finish lunch till 4.30 p.m. We went off to visit a local museum and chateau and both your dear mother and Diana got the giggles very badly and I felt very ashamed as the rather spotty French lady showing us round was clearly getting rather annoyed. I don't suppose your mother's conduct had anything to do with the large amount of wine consumed at lunch. The Gunns had dinner at our hotel and then departed for Caen, Mr Gunn by then talking a great deal of fairly incoherent nonsense. On the Thursday we drove to Cherbourg, having a picnic observed with interest by children from an orphanage and three porky-fat priests. The boat was almost empty but Nidnod found some friends and was able to have a non-stop talk for a couple of hours. We landed at Southampton at 9.30 p.m. and were home an hour later. Cringer was insane with delight to see us back. Your brother is home looking clean (comparatively) healthy and happy. We had drinks (a good many) with the Bomers last night and today James Staples is here for lunch in a new suit and accompanied by a girl-friend, small and shy, who is Lupin's housekeeper, a very odd arrangement.

Best love,

D

A classic Mortimer holiday. My mother made 'bosom friends' with the most random people who would run for the hills when they saw her coming. My father enjoyed recounting strange anecdotes loosely based on his observations.

Budds Farm

Dearest L,

I hope you are in robust health and that you are satisfying Miss Birchnettle (or whatever your Head Mistress is called). Your sister Jane is back from Greece and moves up to Yorkshire at the end of this week. I believe your fond mother is going to drive her up. Jane is shortly due to take her driving test which ought to give at least one hearty laugh to all concerned. Your erratic brother Lupin is down here for one night. Alas, your ever-loving mother is in one of her little moods and has never stopped nagging him and giving him totally unwanted

and very ridiculous advice. The ponies seem to be well; Pongo
has a nasty little itch and Cringer's breath would drive a car.
Moppet has killed many sleepy mice. I was very lame one day
and had to take some disgusting pills which made me feel sick.
Caroline Blackwell stayed here for a night and the Bomers
and Parkinsons came to Dinner. Your mother talked without
ceasing and no one else got a word in. Your mother starts
her bridge lessons on Monday. I shall be mildly surprised if
she keeps them up. We had dinner last night at that pub in
Overton where I once took you. Do you still like your new
dormitory? I trust you are kind to the unfortunate new girl!

Best love,

D

*The unfortunate new girl, Kate Evans, becomes my best
friend and with no family in England she is welcomed with
open arms by both my parents as a surrogate daughter.*

The Sunday Times
30 September

Dearest Lumpy,

Thank you for your letter. You seem to be having some
curious adventures. I hope you are doing some work and
that you are approaching your examinations in a spirit of
well-justified confidence. I have been at Newmarket for most
of the week. Mrs Hambro arrived at Cousin Tom's house in
a new sports Mercedes that would have turned your barmy

brother Lupin green with envy. My friend Mr Barling was kicked in the back by a yearling at the Sales and is in hospital with severe injuries. Cringer was very pleased to see me when I got home; Pongo and your dear mother rather less so. Your mother has been in Yorkshire assisting your sister Jane to move house. The new woman at the cottage, whose name eludes me, seems pretty scatty. As regards your holiday skiing; yes, you can go provided I approve of the expense involved (you have so far afforded me no information on that fairly important point). Also I wish to know with whom you are going and who is in charge of the party. I do not want a lot of giggling girls on their own making sheep's eyes at the handsome instructors. You and Charlotte together would constitute a threat to decorum and commonsense. An elderly lady I know has just had all her jewellery swiped by a burglar, including a string of pearls about twice the length of a bicycle chain. There is to be a 'Sunday Times' exhibition at the National Gallery from Oct 22 for 6 months. Some of my books will be on view which ought to attract visitors in their thousands. I hope you will attend the exhibition in a suitably respectful frame of mind.

Best love,

D

I have started at Tudor Hall but my old school friends from Daneshill are planning a skiing trip.

As my father predicted we did not behave with due decorum. On the train home I became seriously ill and the second we arrived in England I was rushed into hospital with acute appendicitis.

1972

Dearest L,

Are you really coming home next week? I'm glad you have warned me in time. I will put everything of value in the bank, nail down the carpets, and go off to Brighton for three days. I will leave a couple of tins of Kitticat for you to share with Moppet. Mind you divide them up fairly and don't pinch the bigger helping. Your mother is hunting today and I trust that for once she will avoid a painful accident. I nearly ran over a fox on the M4 last night. Cringer is in great form and is becoming more cunning than ever. Farmer Luckes is going to retire, so he says, at the end of the year and build himself a bungalow. Mr Hicks's old father died suddenly when drinking a cup of tea last Wednesday. He was over 80. A man shot a policeman in Newbury last Friday but luckily did not kill him. I went to a dinner party in London given by Schweppes and consumed about a ton of caviar. I have got three parties in London next week. I have no news of your sister Jane but I believe Paul is off to Liverpool for a fortnight. I saw Aunt Pam yesterday wearing a really hideous magenta hat. She really does get hold of some very peculiar clothes. I think she must go round all the local jumble sales.

Best love,

D

The appalling dress sense of Aunt Pam (aka The Hamburger) was only slightly better than that of my father.

Budds Farm
26 February

Dearest L,

I hope you got back safely and have settled down to hard work and good behaviour! Your plump sister Jane and your skinny brother Lupin are due down here today. Your ever-loving mother is hunting and I, as usual, am working. I have given your mother a record player for her birthday. I hope you see my photograph in Horse and Hound this week as I'm sure you will agree I am far better-looking than the picture, taken just after the completion of a heavy lunch, suggests. Pongo is very smelly today so I am banishing him out of doors for a breath of fresh air. On Thursday I am off to a champagne and oysters party in the morning and then to a big lunch party at the Savoy afterwards. I wish you were coming with me. Or do I? I am hoping to get a new car in June, a BMW. What colour do you think would be agreeable? I fancy the fashionable dog-sick yellow or a bright, vivid red like Crosse and Blackwell's tomato soup. If you leave sweet papers lying about in my new car, I shall be reluctantly compelled to request you to ride in the boot.

If you can't be good be careful.

'Safety first, safety first, look before you leap.

One false step, if you don't think twice,

Bang goes your motto and mother's advice!'

etc etc.

xx D

Dad decided on a vivid tomato red BMW.

Budds Farm

Dearest L,

I hope you are in rude health and are not eating too much. Do you weigh 11 stone yet? Your dear mother is totally immersed in this ghastly local election in which she is a candidate. Talk about flaps! I don't know what she will do if she is beaten as she may well be as her opponent is very popular and has lived here a long time. Cringer is very well and sends you a big wet kiss backed by slightly smelly breath. We had the Parkinsons and Roper-Caldbecks to dinner – not very original or exciting. The Bomers are still in Minorca. Val Haslam is leaving to go and work in Newmarket. No news of your unpredictable brother Lupin but your lively sister

Jane seems quite happy in Harrogate. I am off to Newmarket for 3 days next week, leaving on Thursday, the day after the election. Brigadier Gerard is running his last race on Saturday. He is now worth about two and a half million pounds. Nice work if you can get it!!

    Best love,

    D

My father tries to educate me about outstanding racehorses, which is slightly more interesting than my mother's council elections.

    Brigadier Gerard's owners and breeders John and Jean Hislop, great friends of my parents, were two of the more entertaining characters in the racing world. Jean Hislop's outrageous behaviour, both on and off the racecourse, always amused my father.

    On Brigadier Gerard's final appearance he defeated Riverman by one-and-a-half lengths to win his second Champion Stakes. He retired at the end of his four-year-old season, a winner of seventeen races from eighteen starts.

The Sunday Times
29 October

Dearest Lumpy

    I hate Sundays. They really do depress me. Yesterday we went to a wedding at Wantage, a very pretty girl called Selina Meade, whose mother is an old girl friend of mine and who has presented her husband with no sons but six pretty and charming daughters. The reception was in a large marquee and luckily it was a warm, sunny afternoon. The flowers had to be seen to be believed. Your mother wore a purple hat and talked incessantly, few people hearing a single word she said. The evening before, Gypsy Lola and her husband, who is slightly cross-eyed, came to dinner. There was a lot of boring talk about the Garth Hunt. I just switched my mind off and thought of other things. There are a lot of rats here but the dogs and the cat are too overfed, lazy and stupid to catch any. I have no news of your sister Jane or your brother Lupin but very often no news is good news. You will be highly amused to hear that your slightly gaga father has been awarded a prize for being the outstanding racing journalist of the year (Loud cheers and some muffled laughter). I get presented with the ghastly thing at a large lunch (300 people) in London and look forward to the whole thing about as much as a visit to a Pakistani dentist. Anyway, to celebrate what would otherwise be a dreary incident, I am enclosing a small present. Don't spend it all on gin and improper magazines if you please. I trust Snouter is well and that you are looking after him as he is subject to colds from November onwards. Can it be true that you are coming home soon? If so, I think I will take a long weekend in Brighton.

Best love,

D

My father – always self-deprecating, even about the most serious of issues – is presented with the Clive Graham Memorial Trophy for racing journalist of the year.

The Sunday Times
25 November

Dearest Lumpy,

Thank you so much for your birthday card which I liked very much. I do hope you are having good fortune in your examinations papers and have not made too many gigantic blots on your answers. By the way, I simply cannot remember if I told you that Lord Belper was very pleased with the card you sent him and wishes you to give 2 lumps of sugar to Leo on his behalf. Your sister Jane came down here for a night, ate a lot and seemed in good form. I had to go to a big dinner in London last Wednesday. Princess Anne made a speech and was really quite amusing. Driving back through Newbury at 1.30 a.m. I was stopped by the police. They were making a check for stolen cars and I was NOT breathalysed. I have given Nidnod ear-rings for her silver wedding present; pearls with diamonds round them. She seems very pleased. Cousin Tom has given us a lovely ice bucket in which the ice keeps for a day or so. Last night we had a very good dinner with the Mayhew Saunders. I had Sarah Bomer on one side which was good but a truly tedious lady on the other. Tomorrow we have a singularly unpromising luncheon for Nidnod's hunting friends. One of the papers I write for is sending me a dozen bottles of champagne to celebrate winning the Derby award which is nice of them. I will keep a bottle for you and Emma in the holidays.

I bought a new toaster yesterday, only to return home and find Nidnod had bought an identical one in London.

Give my love to Kate. Cringer sends you a big, wet, slightly smelly kiss.

    Best love,

    D

Lord Belper, without doubt my father's most disreputable friend, was a good laugh. He would encourage me to recite rude poems I had picked up from my dad. 'If skirts get any shorter, said the walrus with a sob, there will be two more cheeks to powder and a bit more hair to bob.'

'Chez Nidnod'
Sunday, 3 December

Dearest Lumpy,

    I hope you are big and well and looking, as usual, like a plump Dutch cheese. How are the O levels going? Have you been caught cribbing yet? I took your mother to Newmarket last week. In the town she put the key of my car into the lock upside down, tried to force it and broke it in half. I could not get another key and the car was immobilised for 48 hours. Thanks very much! We are all rather sad here as Mrs Henderson, whose daughter was at Daneshill, fell on the road out hunting last Tuesday and died soon afterwards. The new people were supposed to be moving into the cottage today but never turned up. Not a very good sign! How did the Tudor Hall bazaar go? Is it true that a shortsighted lady tried to purchase you under the misapprehension that you were a stuffed meat-ball? Your mother was hunting today and got very wet. I cannot tell you other details as I dozed off while she was recounting her exploits. Cringer came racing with me this afternoon and ate 10p worth of chocolate on the way back. I played bridge with old Lord Carnarvon on Thursday. He plays, if anything, rather worse than your mother does which is saying a great deal. Tomorrow we have lunch with Nika the Squeaker.

Best love,

D

My poor mother was frustrated that my father took very little interest in her hunting exploits. These often involved the horse falling – it was never an option that she had fallen off the horse.

Budds Farm

Dearest L,

I hope you are well and not giving the Head Mistress too much trouble. What a revolting story you told me! I suppose you learnt that from one of your delightful friends at Tudor Hall. You ought to be strung up and flogged with bunches of nettles and thistles! Last night I had to go to Frimley and lecture to members of the Garth and South Berks. Your dear mother told me it was a smart affair and made me put on evening clothes, while she was decked out as if she was off to a Ball at Buckingham Palace. On arrival I found she had got in a muddle (nothing new in that) and everyone else was dressed as for a wet afternoon at Tweseldown! Rather embarrassing, don't you think? However I think my little talk went down all right. We had quite a good supper and your poor mother was sick this morning. Moppet made a gigantic mess during the night in your poor mother's bath. On Thursday we went to Charlie Jamieson's wedding reception. He has married a girl like a twittering bird. Jane was there and was very put out because someone thought I was her husband! I gave dinner to Jane, Paul and Gale afterwards. Jane ate and drank as much as ever and is smoking so much her lungs must be like an unswept factory chimney. I am off to Sandown today where I am judging a competition for the best turned-out horse with sweet Mary Gordon-Watson. Your mother does not want to go to Corfu (why?) so I am now thinking of Rhodes or Crete. A helicopter crashed near here yesterday and two people were killed. Lady Darling turned up in the afternoon. She had been to a funeral wearing a dress she bought for 40p at a jumble sale. I don't think it was cheap at the price. The funeral had been of a cousin of Uncle Ken's shot in Ulster. You may have seen pictures of it in the paper. Is it true Bernadette Devlin was at Tudor Hall a few years ago and captain of the lacrosse team?

xx

My father hated standing out in any way, so a big faux pas for him was turning up at an event in his best bib and tucker and finding the other guests in casual wear. Nidnod gets the blame again.

1973

Budds Farm
27 April

Dearest L,

I suppose your pillow has been soaked with tears as you lie in bed and think of the old folks (or is 'soaks' the more appropriate word) at Home. I miss you here as the house is tidier and the plug has been pulled in my loo. Your poor mother got ticked off by Aunt Pam for arriving late on Tuesday. Those two sisters!! Cringer slept almost on my pillow that night and I would have relished his company more had not his breath smelled strongly of rather ancient fish. I trust you will work hard this term. Take some exercise, too, and try and get into the Lacrosse fifteen or the football eleven or something like that. I will come down with a big smoked salmon picnic as soon as the weather is a bit warmer. Bring Snouter with you and one or two really cheeky friends. I met the toad in the herbaceous border again this morning and we are becoming friends. He has a crafty look so I address him as Harold Wilson. Cringer is very popular at the Carnarvon Arms where he dances for cold sausages. I had lunch at Ascot yesterday with old Lord Carnarvon and his bird who is about Jane's age but not such a vast eater. I hear there is a beach at Corfu reserved for nudists. What price Emma landing up there?

Best love,

D

I loved going on picnics with my father, always a jolly affair. After one such picnic the school matron caught him doing the sailor's hornpipe down the passage wearing my school boater.

Budds Farm

Dearest L,

Not much news from here except a cow got into the garden and did a lot of damage. Also an objectionable mole is creating much havoc and an elderly thrush elected to expire just outside the front door. Your brother is now living in London and I HOPE he manages to stay out of trouble! Your dear mother is flapping like an over-excited hen about various things to do with the Garth Hunt and I am expected to listen to her tales of woe and frustration. Your Aunt is back from Corfu and apparently enjoyed herself. When do you come home next so that I can lock up the silver and go away? How did you get on in your examinations? If you did badly, I shall probably export you to work in the salt mines in Poland so just WATCH IT!! The weather continues chilly, too cold even for croquet. I have not been able to wear my new leopardskin bathing pants yet.

The new car continues to go well and is much admired by one and all. I have no news from Jane but assume she is still alive, not having heard anything to the contrary. Everything in the garden is horribly backward and the strawberries do not look like ripening till the autumn. There seems to be a good crop of raspberries. What a pity they upset your stomach and you will in consequence be unable to consume any. I will ask your dear mother to provide a health-giving junket for you instead.

Best love,
D

In a moment of madness I had given Dad a pair of skimpily fitting leopardskin bathing trunks – they did not go down well. A few weeks later I caught him trying to palm them off on Mr Randall, the gardener.

1976

Budds Farm

Dearest L,

I was very pleased to hear from you and I hope you are surviving the heat-wave and the novel experience of having to do some work. I expect it is dull for you down here but I sincerely hope you will come and visit your aged parents occasionally. You are always welcome, particularly if you can give a little notice of your impending arrival. As I am very old-fashioned in my ideas on the conduct of life, I would like to know quite clearly your position vis à vis Henry. Of course if you elect to live together there is nothing I could do about it even should I desire to do anything. But since I am your father and you are only eighteen, I would like to know more or less what the set-up is. Perhaps Henry would be kind enough to come down one day and explain his plans and what he visualises happening in the future. I think it would be only civil to your mother and to myself. I do not grudge you any happiness you may derive from your current arrangement and I am not in the habit of applying moral standards that have largely ceased to exist. All the same, I do feel a certain responsibility towards you, and apart from which I love you very much and have no wish to see you hurt. I had a long talk with Loopy the other day and he is far from happy about the way things are at present. That, however, is a matter for Henry to settle.

Pongo collapsed after a walk the other day. Luckily I revived him with cold water and was not compelled to administer the kiss of life. Your mother's trip to Jersey was fraught with drama and one member of the party achieved the rare feat of breaking his ankle while doing a pee. Lucky it was only his ankle! A local lady has been bitten by an adder (on the Forestry Land where I go with the dogs) and is in a parlous plight. I had lunch with the B-Atkins on Sunday. They sent you their love and Rosamund is keen to meet you. Mark and William went to the Test Match and enjoyed seeing the streaker! Last night I took your mother to Longparish and gave that saucy rook a bag of nuts. He enjoyed the paper bag slightly more than the nuts. Lupin was here yesterday; he seems to be doing some rather peculiar jobs.

Best love,

R

My brother Lupin persuaded me to buy a vomit-coloured Fiat from a job lot of twelve that he had purchased from a bankrupt coach company, no mean feat as I did not drive let alone have a driving licence. His original offer of 'buy two get one free' was not of great appeal. By then Henry had been my boyfriend for almost a year and had already

been given the nickname 'Hot Hand Henry' by my father
for obvious reasons. Luckily, or unluckily depending from
whose point of view, he had just passed his driving test
and so we set off for a camping/fishing holiday in Scotland.
Miraculously the car got us there and back. Instead of
returning to my parents' home afterwards, we drove to
London and shacked up in a friend's house in Fulham.

My parents' hopes that I join the Foreign Office are dashed.
Instead Charlie Shearer (my brother's most disreputable
friend) gives me a job working as a general dogsbody in a
massive junk shop in Fulham called the Furniture Cave.

Budds Farm
24 October

Dearest Miss Plumpling,

A lot of people are coming to lunch and your dear mother
is in a fine old flap. Lupin has gone to Derbyshire, looking
rather yellow and with eyes like badly poached eggs, in
the company of C. Hurt who is very pale and whose face
now resembles a crumpled towel. Jane is apparently renting
a country house with wall-to-wall carpeting and a large
garden. Mrs Bomer has bought a new car; the colour is that
of the messes made by dogs after de-worming pills. How
is the revolting Chappie? Not too exuberant, I trust. Mr
P. is back home after his kidney operation and feels weak.
This afternoon I am visiting the Surtees in their new house
at West Ilsley. The Income Tax Authorities are pursuing me

with a relentlessness worthy of a nobler cause. I reply with insults and post-dated cheques later cancelled. Prison looms. Moppet was very sick yesterday after emitting three blood-curdling screams. Your great-aunt stayed here and is as deaf as a telegraph pole. The TV had to be turned on at maximum volume and gave me fearful headaches. Your mother was kissed by The Mayor of Basingstoke and called 'Darling Cynthia' when in an intoxicated condition (The Mayor, not Nidnod). She has had her hair done three times since and has bought some gaudy new clothes. Can you beat it? She got sloshed the other night and gave a monologue on religion that went on till 1 a.m. I went to bed at 11 p.m: the guests were too polite to do so. More fools them, I say.

Kind regards to H.

Love,

D

My parents' dinner guests are a captive audience for my mother's current obsessions and grievances. She is clearly firing on all cylinders and convinced that she is the talk of Hampshire after her encounter with the Mayor of Basingstoke. Not exactly Sean Connery.

The Old Ice Box
3 November

Dearest L,

V cold here and Nidnod is bedridden with a vicious

brand of catarrh. We were asked to go away this weekend to Newmarket but declined. The whole business of packing up, coping with the dogs etc is too arduous. Old Queen Mary, when she spent a weekend with chums, used to take dressers, one footman, one page, two chauffeurs, one Lady in Waiting, one maid for the Lady in Waiting, and one detective. The Lady in Waiting wrote beforehand to request for a chair to be placed outside the Queen's bedroom on which the footman or page sat all night: fresh barley water every two hours during the day; ice in the bedroom at 11.30 p.m; 6 clean towels every day. The Queen brought her own sheets and pillow cases.

The annual Budds Farm shoot took place on Wednesday and was a great success. Three pheasants were mown down, in varying stages of mobility, between the rubbish heap and the bottom end of the croquet lawn; after which the guns, or more accurately the gun, a boy of fifteen, retired for a cup of mazawatee tea and crumpet, or more accurately, crumpets.

Did you know (why should you?) that the last occasion that someone in France was eaten by a wild wolf was October 1918? In some remote parts of France there is still an 'officier de louveterie' or officer responsible for wolves. In some French regiments there is an 'officier colombophile' or officer in charge of carrier pigeons! Here is another piece of valuable information: eggs produced by pond ducks are much nastier than the eggs of running water ducks.

Farmer Luckes has had another stroke and is v groggy. A lady in Newbury has strangled her ever-loving husband with a dressing-gown cord. A row is going on about the proposed

Highclere by-pass. If the alternative route is chosen, lorries will pass where our stable is now.

I see Blue Circle Cement is closing down several branches. I hope Loopy will not be made redundant. I hear betting shops are making a fortune in S. Wales and the North East where workers have been given fat redundancy payments. As the old song goes, 'Cocktails and Laughter, what comes after? Nobody knows.' I have sold Padro as a stallion which is a bit of luck. Christmas draws hideously close. As I have often said before, my ideal Christmas would be spent in a Jewish hotel in Eastbourne. Mabel, my old Nanny, rang up yesterday. She is 88 and completely on the ball. Her daughter, who held a good job in the Bank of England, has bought a small estate in Dorsetshire.

Love to all, x

My father enlightens me on his idea of an ideal Christmas.

Budds Farm

Dearest L,

I trust you are all thriving. Your Mother is up in Northumberland and I hope the change will do her good. She was a bit overwrought in Ascot week and was very tired by the end of it. One night at dinner we had the well known door slamming act followed by a brief speech in which she expressed the fervent wish that my final departure from this vale of tears would not be long delayed. The guests looked slightly surprised but gallantly went on pecking away at the tinned prawns in rice. Lupin's god-father Fitz Fletcher stayed here. Not long ago he went with his daughter to a party in Somerset. There were 53 guests and fifty developed acute food poisoning from the curried turkey. They were very ill indeed and six were in 'intensive care' for a week. Ascot was quite fun but it is getting shoddy. The Royal Enclosure lawn might be the Mayor's annual garden party at Basingstoke. The clothes were dowdy and the number of pretty, well turned out girls could have been counted on the horns of a goat. We had lunch one day with Jamie Crichton Stuart and his wife. Luckily I found an ex-girlfriend there and had a cosy time on a sofa. Your mother cornered an elderly woman and favoured her with a lecture on hepatitis. On Saturday I lunched with the Beaumonts at Ascot, got slightly sloshed and made what I now realize were some highly unsuitable remarks. I saw James Staples looking unbelievably clean and smart in the Royal Enclosure. Stephen Willett is doing Hotel Management and Catering at Surrey University. He heard there was a waiter shortage at Ascot and offered his services. He was detailed to serve in the private chalet hired by Mr. K. Abdullah who has several oil wells at the bottom of his garden. Mr Abdullah took a fancy to him and at the end of the afternoon gave him a little tip of £50. In addition Stephen got £18 in wages for the day. Nice work if you can get it. Tiny Man has just rolled in a singularly repulsive mess and I must give him a bath. There was a 15 mile queue into Newbury on Saturday for the air display. Dean Swift wrote: 'I am grown so hard to please that I am offended with every unexpected face I meet where I visit, and the least Tediousness or Impertinence gives me shortness of breath and a pain in the stomach.'

Kind Regards to H.

Best Love,

R

P.S. Your Mother and I had tea with Mr Abdullah. I enjoyed seeing your mother in full flood of verbosity with him as he understands English about as well as I understand Arabic. There was a rather sinister man there, a combination of valet, chauffeur and armed bodyguard.

Language was a meaningless barrier to my mother once she got the bit between her teeth.

1977

Hullo Fatchops!

Thank you for your saucy Valentine which was much appreciated. How is the cooking going? Can you make clear gravy soup without great eyes of grease winking up at you from the plate: fishcakes that do not crumble at the first fork-prod yet actually contain fish: and rice pudding with a brown top that does not taste like very old brown paper? I expect Henry is already putting on weight. How is his stomach, by the way? Nidnod is no barmier than usual but just carries on doing and saying the most extraordinary things. She had a drink with the Gaselees on Sunday and dropped a cigarette on their best sofa, burning a hole in the cover. Some French people were there who talked faultless

English. Nidnod insisted on addressing them in a series of weird sounds that she imagined had some connection with the French language. Needless to say no one could understand what she was getting at and I was covered with mortification and confusion. Pongo's inside is in poorish order and his output of really appalling smells has been increased to an almost unbearable level. Poor Lupin. Most of his friends now seem to be in prison; others doubtless ought to be. They are a very seedy collection of social misfits. Not much news from here. Mrs Black appears to be shacking up with an eighteen year old moron whose father keeps the chemists shop at Kingsclere. I criticise her conduct not from the point of view of morals but of taste. People are so apt to confuse the two. Sarah Bomer's mother is very ill and Sarah has had to go down to Wales to help her father. I saw a huge rat near the stables yesterday. It leered at me in a manner I found distinctly objectionable. I resent that attitude from members of the animal kingdom. No news from your sister, the ever-popular Hexham housewife and culture queen. I suppose she is still busy laying carpets at Scroggs's Bottom or whatever her new semi-detached chateau on the Tyne is called. I hear the ghastly Shearer has been married in America. I dare say the lady of his choice will soon be regretting her rashness. I would not trust him as far as I could throw a full size piano.
XXX D

Having given Henry food poisoning twice, not intentionally, my parents generously pay for me to do a cordon bleu cookery course.

My father is mortified by Nidnod's erratic behaviour, not

for the first time. When she insists she speaks French fluently,
which she clearly does not, he would make a quick exit,
leaving other people bemused and amused.

The Old Nuthouse
Burghclere
26 February

My Dearest L,

Now that you and Henry are formally engaged, I send
you both my sincere good wishes for your future happiness.
Marriage can be a bit tricky. So many people expect to
be blissfully happy: they do very well indeed if they end
up reasonably contented, a situation most likelifully to be
achieved if the wife cooks well and does not talk too much,
and if the husband is out of the house for most of the day and
has not got enough money to cut a dash with other women. I
hope there will be no family arguments prior to the wedding
though at present the omens seem not altogether favourable.
If disagreements arise, I suggest they are settled by Loopy and
myself who are both fairly tolerant and easygoing. If things
are left to Nidnod and Lady Kennard, I fear that sparks,
possibly more solid objects, may start flying. The further
apart they remain, the better. Telephone conversations, too,
must be discouraged.

I hope you will get married down here but that of course
is up to you. If you have a church wedding and a formal
reception, Henry must wear a tail coat! He can easily hire

one from Moss Bros or from his brother's Eton tailor. He will not need a hat. A grey top hat at a wedding is very non-U. I certainly do not wish him to follow the example of Paul who wore cornflower-blue velvet and looked like Little Boy Blue going off to blow his horn.

Once you have decided where the nuptial rites are to be celebrated, I will look out for suitable caterers. The number of people to be asked will depend on the price charged per head.

I only hope all closely concerned with this ritual tribal function will still be on speaking terms by the time the day arrives. Much tolerance and goodwill may be required.

Best love,

RM

I don't care for weddings but I may look in for a drink.

Excellent marriage advice from Dad, I don't think.

Budds Farm
22 April

Dearest L,

Thank you for your letter. I did not greatly relish my 24hr sojourn in the Winchester Clinic, a singularly dreary edifice conducted on Spartan lines. Not long before my operation a nurse came in and handed me a sort of nightdress with strings on that she told me to wear. Anything to oblige, so I put it on and tied it up securely. When the nurse came back she had hysterics as I had put the ruddy thing on back to front and she could not get the strings untied, eventually half the staff of the clinic including a cook was engaged in trying to undress me. The operation took 45 minutes and needed 18 stitches and I was quite sleepy afterwards but happily your Mother turned up at teatime, bundled me into her car in my pyjamas and drove me home. Was very sore for a day or two but that is wearing off. The Lemprière-Robins are staying here with Emma. We had other people for the week-end and a dinner party at which the food was below standard. Lupin is in good form so perhaps his latest pills have done some good. I have just ordered some wine from my bookmaker – cheap and fairly nasty. We hope to go to France for a week in May – somewhere in Brittany, I think. We must now go and buy some haddock.

Best love to all, D

My father had been in hospital for the day having a malignant melanoma removed. We are at a loss to explain how a man who ran the radio service in the POW camps is incapable of putting on a hospital robe the correct way round. Thank goodness for all concerned he had on his boxer shorts.

Budds Farm
6 May

Dearest L,
    V cold and wet here. As regards your wedding, my advice

is to make the service as simple as possible. There will not be many people in the church and half of them will not sing, so don't have a lot of hymns. In particular no LONG hymns. Not more than 3 or 4 verses otherwise people get bored and it will just be an organ solo! Don't be too ambitious over music. The organist probably plays with one finger.

Everything is fixed up with the caterers who seem efficient. XX RFM

My father's ideas for the wedding are not always the same as my own. He wants to opt for a short service including a couple of rousing hymns, followed by a reception at Newbury racecourse where meat paste sandwiches and a glass of Co-op sparkling wine would be served. Not forgetting his motto that a good speech is a short one.

Budds Farm
11 May

Dearest L,

I hope you are fully recovered after what was doubtless a fatiguing week-end. There certainly seems to have been plenty of incident! Your mother arrived back with a strange man who stayed the night. I wonder who he was. I gather your mother had the best of three falls with Mrs Carew and I strongly suspect that both were well and truly sloshed. Mrs Carew does not seem to fancy you very much but I hope you will not be required to see a lot of her in the future. It is

very wet and cold here and Pongo has got the shivers. I hope
arrangements for the wedding are going well. We must keep
your mother and Mrs C. well apart at the reception. Can it
be true that the best man is going to wear a kilt? I don't take
weddings all that seriously but I don't want him to come in
fancy dress and mob the whole thing up completely. I trust
Henry is behaving himself and has not destroyed many more
of his employers' cars.

Best love,
D

*We had agreed to have an engagement party in Devon, even
though we had in fact married secretly a year before. My
father very sensibly did not attend and was happy to avoid
what turned out to be an interfamilial debacle with fists and
fur flying.*

Budds Farm
22 May

My Dearest L,

The news of your marriage naturally comes as a considerable shock to me. I accept the situation that you have both
created and will make the best of it but my acceptance does
not mean that no wounds have been inflicted. It is hurtful
that you chose to go and get married – one of the most
important occasions in your life – without wishing your
parents, who love you deeply, to be present, and without

even having the grace to inform them. It was in particular a cruel thing to do to your mother and you surely realised the pain it would cause her. Having got married, you maintained a deception for nearly eighteen months. It is not agreeable for me to realise that Henry has constantly been a guest in my house while at the same time deceiving me in cold blooded fashion in respect of my daughter. Such conduct inevitably sows the seeds of mistrust for the future. As for the 'wedding', most of those who attend the reception will know you have made asses of your parents just as Henry has made asses of his, and inevitably we shall all feel a bit foolish. It is your mother and I who have to do all the explaining to relations and close friends who can hardly be expected to applaud your conduct. I can understand your desire to be married: what I cannot condone is the prolonged deception that followed. I do not know how Henry's family will take it. They have every reason to be angry and you can hardly expect them to take a more affectionate view of yourself. If there are repercussions from Devonshire, you have only yourselves to blame.

I hope if possible never to refer to this distasteful matter again. I wish you every possible happiness in your married life which, through your own folly has got off to a thoroughly unsatisfactory start.

Your loving father,
RM

On the whole I like to think I was well behaved when I was young (at least, compared to Lupin). However, at the age of nineteen I secretly married my boyfriend Henry at Fulham

Registry Office. HHH was sworn to secrecy and astonishingly, despite his habitual indiscretion when under the influence, my parents never found out.

A year later, shortly before what was to be our proper wedding we had to tell them the truth. Both my parents were extremely shocked and upset. It would be an understatement to say my father was not HHH's greatest fan from the beginning of the relationship. When the drama had died down my affinity returned to that of the youngest sibling and throughout my marriage Dad showed me nothing but support and affection.

Burghclere
11 June

Dearest L,

How are things going down your way? I have ordered (and paid for) 96 bottles of Louis Kremer White Label Champagne and hope that will be enough. I think there has been a present sent to you here – a cushion – from the first Mrs Surtees. Answers to the invitations are flooding in. All the refusals – a high proportion – are from people in Devonshire, presumably relations and friends of Henry and his family. You will be pleased to hear Aunt Boo is coming! Your mother has had a fairly stiff letter from Mrs Pope which she is sending on to you as it is only right and proper that you both know what our old friends feel about the whole business. Lupin has been ill with dysentery while staying with the Guinnesses. Major

Surtees crowned the Jubilee Queen of West Ilsley and then fell off the platform, injuring the right cheek of his arse.

Your affec. father,

RM

My poor father is on the receiving end of yet more disapproval from various friends and family.

Dearest L,

It was nice seeing you and I hope you will behave yourself and keep well in the interval before the 'wedding'. I have written to Loopy and told him that a suit, not a tailcoat is the correct order. Henry will no doubt do what he likes and if he turns up in leopard jock strap it is nothing to do with me. I would of course prefer him to conform. Be tactful with your mother as she is in a very nervous state and liable to make scenes. After all, you have put a great strain on her.

RM

My father gives implicit instructions that, in lieu of a speech, the following will be sung by the Mortimer family at the reception (tune: 'How pleasant to know Mr Lear'):

> *How pleasant to know Lady K,*
> *My ideal of a wife and a mother,*
> *Her last husband called it a day*
> *But very soon she picked up another.*

As for Henry I freely admit
That I find him a little bit wearing.
It's not that he is really a shit
But when pissed he is so overbearing.
I am leaving the best to the end,
That fearful old harridan, Granny,
If I catch her one day on the bend
I'll give her my boot up the fanny.

As this is a fairly respectable collection of my father's letters,
I have left out the middle lines of the poem as I do not want
to be sued.

Budds Farm
14 June

Dearest L,

Mrs Rumbold rang up this morning and asked if you had 'a list' anywhere: I said I thought Peter Jones. I hope I was right. May I respectfully offer some advice? When you receive a wedding present, sit down at once and write a short note thanking the donor. Older people, I fear, mind frightfully if they do not receive an acknowledgement in quickish time; in any case, you don't want to be left with a whole stack of letters to be written. I have already heard rumblings from old Camilla about a blanket, and also from my sister about something or other. I agree old people are pernickety and difficult, but if you deal with them speedily, they won't bother me and your mother! God knows, we have plenty to worry about without additional nagging from septuagenarians. Answers to invitations come in at a rapid rate, mostly refusals, thank God, so with luck the drink will last out. I think there has only been 1 (one) acceptance from Lady Kennard's list. I would not myself much fancy driving from Devonshire on a Saturday in July. Your god-father Cecil cannot come, nor, thank God can Gershom Stewart. Aunt Pam has sent a post-card from Monte Carlo where it is cold and wet.

Your affec. father,
RM

Dad is on a roll now with his wedding advice.

Dearest L,

It is incredibly vulgar to address people like Cousins Tom and Cecil Langton-May as 'Mr' on the envelope. T. F. Blackwell Esq or Cecil Langton-May Esquire is correct. 'Mr' is OK for a tradesman.

Xx D

Having taken my father's advice on thank you letters, I get into more trouble for incorrectly addressing the envelopes. A major faux pas.

The Grumblings
Much Chattering
Berks
1 August

Dearest Miss Plumpling,

The rain is pouring down and I am doing my accounts, a task that always reduces me to tears. Yesterday I took the merry Nidnod on a little expedition down the River Avon which she enjoyed. I also bought Christmas presents for you, Jane and Nicholas so that's something off what remains of my mind. Monday was for once fine and we had lunch in the garden. Mr P. honoured us with his presence and bought an agreeable blonde divorcée whom I rather fancy stands a fairish chance of becoming Mrs P. IV! The previous day we lunched with the Darlings where Pongo distinguished himself by doing a No 2 on Noel's head. We had a very good lunch preceded by tepid Pimms almost devoid of alcoholic content. In the evening we were held up in Lambourn by the Carnival which rather annoyed your mother. On the Saturday we dined with Dame Anne Parker-Bowles (the only head of the Girl Guides who had her uniform designed in Paris) and your mother sat next to an elderly actor who recently 'died' in a serial called 'The Survivors'. As a matter of fact he had a thrombosis afterwards and very nearly expired in actuality. Your mother rather fancies him and as he lives in Highclere I shall have to watch it a bit. The Cringer did his utmost to eat the postman yesterday and I shall have to keep an eye on his temper with strangers. I don't know where Lupin is: he seems to have no plans for the future. Still, as long as he is happy it does not much matter. The Bomers old bitch has had six puppies while they are on holiday in Wales. I enclose a small goose's neck to help get you to Scotland for your doubtless sorely needed vacation. Don't give your Jewish solicitors roast pork too often for lunch: or pigs' trotters.

Give my kind regards to Henry,
XXX D

Having survived the marriage blessing, life returns to some form of normality. I put my new cooking skills to use working for a firm of Jewish solicitors in the City.

The Olde Dosse House
Burghclere

My Dearest Miss Plumpling,
I hope you are well and above all happy. I went up to London today and spent a laborious morning with my publisher who was born in Fleet but otherwise seems fairly harmless. I met your bossy sister for Lunch at Ladbroke's Club where most of the members wear dark glasses indoors and look like minor characters from *The Sweeney*. Jane ordered smoked salmon mousse (the most expensive item on the card) and something that looked like curried goat. Paul joined us for coffee and brandy. We then all went to Heywood Hill's bookshop where Jane talked much but purchased little. As Major Surtees's office was nearby we next trooped off there and found him in conference with some pissy Dutchmen. We all joined in and

Paul found the senior Dutchman lived next door to his own firm's factory in Holland so everything got v. matey and a biggish hole was made in the Major's port supply. When we bade farewell, the Major gave Jane a love-bite in the neck: rather saucy of him I thought! We then had tea at Paul's club, after which I got on the wrong train at Waterloo. Nidnod can be very peculiar but she is better than the bride's mother at the wedding we have just been to who was totally slosherino and had to lie down during the reception. She got up to see the lucky couple off by helicopter but unfortunately by then had lost her boots!

   XXX RFM

P.S. The Cringer sends a damp and odoriferous kiss.

On the whole my father has a fairly disparaging view of publishers.

Budds Farm
Sunday

Dearest L,

Thank you so much for your letter. I'm pleased to hear you are coming for Christmas and I shall rely on you to keep your mother more or less under control. She has been in one of her most tiresome moods lately and has given Lupin a bad time this weekend. Thank God I am getting increasingly deaf! We are just off to Newbury for a curry lunch party given by Willie Carson and Dick Hern. Your mother is going on to the Lloyd Webbers afterwards to hear some music. I shall have a good sleep after reading about half a page of the Sunday Times. It has been very cold here and I'd like to turn the heating on but it is impermissible to use oil so early in the autumn. I only hope I do not expire from hypothermia. I think I shall go down to Brighton for a few days and stay with Cousin John. It will be less amusing than in the summer as the flat commands a wonderful view of the nudist beach and he has a telescope in his front room. Mr & Mrs Randall had an enjoyable holiday in Austria; last week they were at the Horse of the Year Show. They have a far larkier time than we do.

Best love to you all,
D

Andrew Lloyd Webber being my mother's latest 'best friend' was invited for drinks with his delightful first wife. Unfortunately Chappie, my dog, took a liking to Andrew and attached himself to his leg and had to be physically removed. I am not sure who was the most embarrassed.

1978

The Crumblings
Much Flapping
Wilts

Dearest Lumpy,

Thank you so much for your letter. I hope you have recovered from your fainting fit. I expect it was the result of your condition unless of course you had had your nut in the martini bucket! Who revived you and how? We have a number of people coming to dinner tomorrow and Nidnod is busily engaged doing hideous things to a chicken in the kitchen. Her new machine makes everything taste like old gymshoes cooked in yesterday's washing-up water but I don't dare say so. I went to Salisbury today and had lunch on the river – toasted cheese and onion sandwiches, rather bad for the wind as I soon discovered. Cousin Tom's filly won a £12,000 race at Chester yesterday: she might win the Oaks. Lord Carnarvon's butler-valet-chauffeur-nurse has had a heart attack and the old boy (Lord C, not the butler) is very put out though doubtless the latter is not all that pleased too. Tiny Man is v. restless, there being three bitches on heat within easy walking distance. I had a very vulgar anonymous communication today: I suspect the sender was Major Surtees. Anyway he is going to get a real rasper in reply. Tell Charlotte I will not forget her birthday (I hope) and she can anticipate a small present from her geriatric admirer. I see someone called Carew is involved in a murder at Tavistock. Not, I trust, one of Henry's near-and-dears? A distant cousin of mine was suspected of murdering his ever-loving wife some years back and put his noggin under the wheels of the 3.47 from Maidstone when things were looking rather ugly for him. Later it was discovered that the murderer was in fact a man from near Corbridge who had done in two other people, a cashier from a mine and a Newcastle moneylender.

Kind regards to H.

xxx R

Whilst pregnant with my daughter I could not have oranges in any form or I fainted. Unfortunately I found this out at a drinks party. There was a certain amount of panic as I fell to the floor. My naughty brother suggested to the other guests that there had been a minor earthquake.

Budds Farm
20 August

Dearest Miss Plumpling,

I suppose you are on holiday somewhere and having a really good time. Don't bathe in the sea: you might easily cause a tidal wave. Your mother finally left for Jersey after telling me 27 times what to do with the cat, the greenhouse etc etc. I then went off to recuperate with a quiet week-end chez Surtees: good food and drink, a soft bed and conversation that was sparkling judged by Berkshire standards which could scarcely be lower, comments on the price of bacon at Sainsbury's being the intellectual limit for these parts. Major S saw your brother dining out with a blonde at a trendy SW3 restaurant. Pongo is having ear trouble and never stops shaking his head and making the most horrific smells. We had a barbecue here for the Bomer boys and consumed pork chops and Chianti in a searing north-east wind. William B asked me an improper riddle which I am too shy to repeat. I took Nidnod to lunch at the Fox and Hounds at Crawley: good food but the other people there were dingy beyond belief and looked like provincial income tax inspectors. Mr Cameron is having a ghastly time as apart from having both legs off, his mouth is in a fearful state following radium treatment for cancer. Only a man of exceptional courage could continue to fight for life.

Kind regards to HHH and best love to yourself,
XXX D

Heavily pregnant, the advice still comes thick and fast.

The Old Pork-House
Burghclere

Dearest L,

I hope you are well and looking forward to making your contribution to the population explosion. All fairly quiet here though Nidnod gets over-excited at times. Luckily I am getting increasingly deaf. On Sunday it rained all day. I took Tiny Man to the Dog Show at West Ilsley and he failed to win a prize. In the class for 'Happy Dog with Happy Owner' I was wet to the skin, absolutely miserable and I fear let the side down badly. Your brother revived me with rum and a macaroon. In the evening the Surtees gave a party for 30 in their barn and a good time was had by all; at any rate by me as I made play with a number of recently unmarried women who seemed game for a lark. Perhaps fortunately, your mother had preferred to make her presence felt at the Old Berks Pony Club Camp so for once I felt no need for circumspection, even for decorum. I had a picnic at Goodwood on Tuesday, and on the way back ices and bath buns. Your brother seems to be thriving in his business and with luck he may make enough money soon to afford a hair-cut. At present he is rather like Chappie in human form. We went to a party with the High Sheriff last week: music by the combined orchestras of local schools (I rather fancied a female trombonist) and lots of Berkshire Mayors in awful suits and brass chains round their necks.

Kind Regards to HHH and best love to yourself,
XX D

As my brother Lupin has now turned his talents to driving articulated lorries his long hair is almost as greasy and dirty as his fingernails.

Chez Nidnod
September

Dearest L,

Well done! I hope all goes well and that Henry and Chappie are surviving the strain. Your mother is spinning around like an ancient top and talking a fair amount of nonsense but seems very pleased at having a granddaughter. What are you going to call it (or perhaps her is more polite)? I expect both you and Henry will find nursery life pretty exhausting and the period of night feeds, nappy changing etc etc seems to go on and on. Even at three a child is fairly helpless while a horse may have won the Derby!

My very best love and good wishes and I hope the child will bring you and Henry much happiness.

X

My dad is rarely at a loss when writing. However, when in doubt he refers back to analogies drawn from the more comfortable world of racing.

Chez Nidnod

Dearest L,

I hope all goes well and that you are not over-feeding the baby so that it looks like a balloon. Does it yell much? I expect poor Chappie is very sad without you at home. I made a poor start this morning: when I switched on the Radio the Croydon Salvation Army Band was playing 'Jesus Wants You for a Sunbeam', and when I went to have a bath I had to evict a platoon of exceptionally large and hairy spiders of most menacing aspect. The Surtees went for a holiday in Elba where they own a small villa. They found it had been occupied, vandalised and stripped of all fittings by hippies, mostly Americans. They had to spend a week on hands and knees scrubbing up unspeakable filth. The hippies prowled in the vicinity accompanied by huge and savage dogs. Not much fun for the Surtees! We are just off to drink champagne with the Bomers to celebrate your contribution to the population explosion. How is Henry's stomach? Less restive, I hope. At any rate his trouble is not caused, as Pongo's is, by eating manure! Nidnod is still in very good form and making low whirring noises like a very old top and denoting pleasure.

Best love,

D

It always raised my father's spirits when my mother was on good form. She was delighted to have her first grand-daughter. It was also an excellent excuse to celebrate with our wonderful neighbours the Bomers, who had an endless source of the most delicious vintage champagne.

Chez Nidnod
2 November

Dearest L,

I hope you are all thriving and that Chappie is not making too many messes. I had a fairly hideous day yesterday. I had an appointment in London and accordingly caught the train at Basingstoke, being instructed to go to Platform 4. A train steamed in, I boarded it and immersed myself in The Times. When I looked up, the train was entering Oxford station. I waited 45 minutes for a train to London which was 30 minutes late and then joined a queue for taxis about a mile long. Needless to say I was late for lunch with a man I had never met before and did not much care for when I did. The lunch was fairly nasty. I could not get a taxi to Waterloo afterwards and went by underground in a train in which I was the only white man. There is a large photograph of me in the Newbury News in company with Dick Francis. I am smirking and look an altogether deplorable character. Lupin was here for two nights with stomach ache: he has now departed for Devonshire. We had supper with the Hislops. Mrs H. very sloshed and wore a night dress and no drawers underneath. She talked your mother into stunned silence, no mean achievement. Lord Carnarvon is 80 on Tuesday. We have not been invited to the party for which I am thankful as your mother would have insisted on going. Major Surtees is having a beano for his 60th birthday. I expect we shall go to that. A local lady who lived alone had a stroke and was not discovered for a week. By

then she had been mostly eaten by her dog and her cat.
　See you soon,
　XXX RM

It was well known in the family that nothing gave my father more pleasure that delivering really bad news with suitable gravitas.

Chez Nidnod
Much Shiverings
Berks
12 November

Dearest L,

　Lupin is here with stomach ache and does not look at all well. He is seeing Dr Keeble. He had a bath this morning and must have washed his hair as the bath looked as if a very old moulting retriever had been in it. Your mother is in a very nervy state which makes her a bit tricky after 6 p.m. I have had a filthy cold and wheeze like a tubercular cow. Pongo's stomach is in a poor way and he poisons the atmosphere relentlessly. I have heard of environmental pollution but this is really going a bit too far. I have done some Christmas shopping: your present is v dull but possibly useful. I have sought in Henry's case to appeal to his stomach. Special offers arrive by every post – smoked salmon, a red jersey and four towels, all useful in their various ways. We drove 80 miles to Dorset for lunch yesterday. Luckily I drank too much gin and slept the whole way back. Your mother has a new friend called Mrs Bean: I hear rather too much about her. I hope your daughter is thriving and gets on reasonably well with Chappie. I am slightly fed up with Marlene Dietrich or whatever her name is: she has had some clothes of mine to mend since May and has not started on them yet.

The motor car is at the door.

Good bye, dear friends, no time for more!

Your affec. father,

RM

My father was always sending off for special offers which had often been advertised in such publications as The Field. It was hit or miss as to how successful these purchases were. The red jumper mentioned in his letter was so tight that although he managed to put it on, he needed to cut himself out of it with a pair of nail scissors. He was not best pleased.

Nidnod's Ruin
Burghclere
26 November

Dearest Lumpy,

I hope you are all thriving during this spell of uncouth weather. It would be less disagreeable here if either of the boilers worked. It would not be untrue to say that your mother is slightly barmy at the moment and was convinced that a sausage she was cooking was whipped away by a poltergeist. Mrs Cameron has been staying. She and your mother talked incessantly, neither listening to the other, which is quite sensible as neither said anything worth listening to.

Mrs Randall is giving all her relatives potatoes for Christmas: a sensible and most acceptable present. Would you like a sack of Arran Pilot's or King Edward VII's? I always knew there were some odd people in Devon, but Mr Thorpe and Mr Scott really do take the biscuit with an ease which is almost impertinent. Lupin looks better. His ghastly friend Shearer is back in the country. I regard him as very bad news, even worse than G. Rodney. A man was killed yesterday on the road to Beacon Hill, squashed flat by a huge lorry.

Best love to all, RM x

My mother had already had our house (Budds Farm) exorcised once before when she had insisted there was an alien presence which had, apart from other things, walked noisily up the stairs and shaken her bed in the middle of the night.

1979

Budds Farm
22 January

Dearest L,

Not a very agreeable day here, cold and foggy. Your mother is in very crusty mood so I am trying to keep well out of her way. She has taken a dislike to my dog which is not important but tiresome. I can't say there is much news from this quarter. The strike has not affected the shops in the least and you can buy what you want anywhere without difficulty. Mr Randall has had a nasty cold: Mrs R says he is a silly old man and that he tries to live on strong tea and cigarette smoke. As he is 74 the diet does not seem to have done him much harm. Sarah Bomer and Sylvia Mayhew-Saunders came to lunch: one of them mentioned Pongo and your mother at once disappeared, slamming several doors on the way! Rather silly really at her age. Jane is 30 tomorrow. She will before long be entering the dreaded realm of Old Bagdom, never to return. I gather the weather has been hideous in Northumberland. The Surtees are having a dinner party for 18 in their barn on Saturday: I wonder how many guests will die of hypothermia. We have had a post-card from your brother who seems reasonably happy. I only wish I was with him. The gravediggers are on strike round here so corpses are being shoved into the deep freeze with the fish fingers and the Stork margarine. I hope your daughter is wintering well and maintaining her robust appetite. No sign of the new people moving into the cottage yet. This is an exceptionally dull time of the year and according to your mother I am an exceptionally dull old man, so it would be surprising if this letter was not almost wholly devoid of interest.

Best love,

D

Very sadly Pongo passed away and Nidnod was devastated. My father however, was secretly not completely distraught as the frequently smelly Pongo had been the bane of his life.

Budds Farm
5 February

Dearest L,

I trust that you and Rebecca have recovered from influenza and that Henry is successfully flogging immense quantities of drink to his numerous clients. Life has been fairly dreary here. The fact is that I don't really like this house: it is too big for us and has a thoroughly depressing and unfriendly atmosphere though of course that may be due to the present residents. Also the garden is more than I can now cope with. I would like to move into a hideous but modern bungalow. Your mother seems unable to get over Pongo's death and is liable to get hysterical if his name is mentioned. Mr Randall is in good form: he went up to London last night to watch a TV programme featuring some woman called Ranzen [Esther Rantzen]. At all events, he enjoyed himself. We went to a cocktail party with the Gaselees last Friday: a large number of people in a confined space and I never heard a word anyone said which in fact was not an intolerable deprivation. We had supper at The Swan at Shefford afterwards which is only slightly more expensive than Claridges but they do mushrooms in garlic rather well. Relations between your mother and Aunt Pam remain rather colder than those between Russia and America. I expect they will make it up eventually and then both turn on me and rend me limb from limb. I may come up to London this month as I have been asked to an oyster party at Bentleys and a lunch at the Savoy which will make a change from tinned spaghetti hoops. I really rather envy Lupin in Kenya. I gather he has taken over the hotel motor-boats with the result that none of them are working. I had lunch with Mrs Hislop last Saturday. As a non-stop chatter she is superior even to your mother and talks almost as much balls.

Best love,
D XX

Lupin is blissfully happy on the island of Lamu in Kenya tinkering with boat engines and in the evening reading out my dad's letters to a small audience on the veranda of the Hotel Peponi.

Budds Farm
26 February

Dearest L,

Thank you so much for asking me to the christening and the party afterwards. I enjoyed both of them very much indeed and I think they went off very well. Rebecca behaved with singular decorum. I hope I struck up rather a beautiful friendship with Henry's grandmother but I am not absolutely confident on that point. I trust the photographs came out well! I had a baddish drive home as your mother was very cross and gave me a fearful bashing which continued till she went to bed.

At all events, thank you both very much indeed.

Best love,

RM

Rebecca's christening is the first jamboree that both sides of the family have attended since the marriage blessing. Our best friend and Rebecca's godfather, Andy Loch, kindly allowed us to use his flat in Lennox Gardens for the christening party.

Tuesday

Dearest L,

Very many thanks for your charming porcine card which
I greatly appreciated. We motored up to London yesterday to
go to the Press Derby dinner where I received a presentation.
Those present were for the most part boring and ill-dressed.
The Chairman, Lord Rothermere, made a ghastly speech but
there were rather more entertaining ones by Wilfrid Hyde-
White and Robert Morley. I had a drink beforehand with
Emma E's father and step-mother: they are worried about
E who is swanning about Brazil and no one knows quite
where she is. At dinner Nidnod sat next to a son of the
late Prime Minister, Lord Attlee, who was accompanied by
a lady with lemon coloured hair and a slight impediment in
her speech. Mr A himself was, I think, pissed and achieved
the notable feat of outtalking your mother. I was next to
David Langdon, the cartoonist who does a lot of work
for Punch. I spent a night last week with Cousin John at
Brighton. He has a superb flat overlooking the Marina and
the nudist bathing beach. By a fortunate chance he owns
a huge telescope which he says is for studying the stars.
Douglas Byng came to dinner. He is 87 and used to sing in
drag at the Café de Paris in the nineteen thirties – very funny
and vulgar. He is still very much on the ball and obliged
with 'I'm Milly, a messy old Mermaid' and 'Twenty years a
chambermaid in a house of ill repute'. Peregrine has been
poorly and Nidnod has been in quite a flap. The garden is
very dried up and ugly. We went to a fearful local party and
got nothing to drink bar weak and tepid Pimms. I had a very

coarse post-card from Freddy B-Atkins about Charlotte's engagement.

Love to all from all of us,

D xx

My parents and their friends could be described as many things, boring not being one of them.

Budds Farm
4 August

Dearest L,

Thank you for your interesting letter. All is fairly quiet here though your mother's conduct is liable to be unpredictable after 7 p.m. Audrey does very little work as she and your mother hobnob all morning. Neither of course listens much to the other. No news of Lupin: he is either physically incapable of writing a letter or else he cannot afford a stamp. We went to quite a good lunch party with the Roper-Caldbecks and your mother made sheep's eyes at a very short man called Lloyd Webber. I have just cleaned out The Cringer's run as it was beginning to pong in really alarming fashion. There is not a single apple on any of our fruit trees: all the blossom was destroyed by a late frost. It is going to be a good blackberry year but not a sign yet of any mushrooms. A horse has been stolen from a field in Burghclere: I haven't told your mother or she will start hiring Securicor to protect Jester! There is a big concert in Sydmonton tomorrow but thank God I am not going. The awful thing is that I simply cannot think of anything more to say.

   xx D

When my mother finally found out about the stolen horse she did not hire Securicor. Instead she could be found in her nightie and gumboots with the dogs and an enormous torch doing the rounds several times a night, armed with Lupin's favourite shotgun nicknamed Crippen.

Budds Farm
16 August

Dearest Lumpy,

   I hope you are plump and well and are not finding your work too arduous. Your mother departed on Saturday to stay in Northumberland with Miss Bossy Pants: I have heard nothing since, so assume there haven't been any major dramas. I have been having quite a merry time since as I was out to lunch and dinner on Sunday & also on Monday. It does occur to me that I am invited less for my social charm than because I am regarded as a semi-helpless geriatric who has lost their marbles. I must be getting (have got?) fairly gaga as I crawl out of bed at 7 a.m. and work in the garden before breakfast, cutting down dead rhododendrons and removing brambles and nettles. My arms look as if I had been flogged with barbed wire. I have been doing a little experimental cooking. I drummed up some beef rissoles which looked fairly normal but it needed a hammer and quite a large chisel to dent their surface. At least I have invented a new type of bread. It does not look like bread and it does not really taste much like bread either. An unkind critic might suggest it looks and tastes like a sodden lump of decomposing dough. Mr P. had quite a good holiday down on the Kent coast bar the fact that his daughter got chicken-pox and his au pair girl turned bolo. I think he is restless and would like to move when he retires next year. I suppose he will become Sir Desmond P. when he leaves the Foreign Office. Major & Mrs Surtees are off to Salzburg for the Mozart Festival. They were keen for Nidnod and me to go too, but your mother declined, being as musical as a pair of policeman's bicycle clips. Tiny Man is in very good form but his breath would drive a No 19 bus. Moppet is old and frail, like me. Your cousin Caroline Blackwell is to marry a very rich banker of 41, Tim Holland-Martin. He bred the Derby winner Grundy and has ridden a good many winners at Cheltenham etc. Old Farmer Luckes has been a bit truculent lately and sooner or later he and your mother will have a ghastly row which will be a bore for me as I shall be compelled to listen (several times over) to a blow by blow account.

Best love to you and kind regards to H,
    XXX D
P.S. No news of Lupin who is supposedly due back this week.

Despite senility being one of my father's favourite subjects, he held on to his marbles and continued successfully writing into the last year of his life.

Budds Farm
27 August

Dearest L,

I hope you are all big and well and thriving. I had three days at Rose Cottage where Jane was staying. There were occasional signs of exasperation between Jane and Aunt Pips. Jane never stopped talking, very fast and very indistinctly, and Aunt Pips got browned off as she could not hear half of what Jane said and could not understand the rest. Jane got fed up when she told a long banging story and found that Aunt Pips either had given up listening or had got hold of the wrong end of the stick. We went out for drinks with some people and were rather put out to find a dead dog on the lawn when we left. I think your mother quite enjoyed Jersey. She brought back two crabs which we had for lunch on Sunday. I felt a teeny bit sick afterwards. Two geese came into the kitchen and made a ghastly mess. I have had a v. rude postcard from France with a very cheeky message in French. I have no idea who sent it. Your mother thinks I have a French lover which unfortunately is not the case. Lupin drops in here every now and then. I gave him dinner at the Riviera which is now extremely expensive. The geese have eaten all my flowers and I can't wait to have them killed and shoved into the deep freeze.

Best love to you all,
XX RM

It was always a pleasure staying with my Great Aunt Pips. She had certain similarities to Dr Evadne Hinge of Hinge and

Bracket. She had an amazing musical ear; hearing a piece of music once she could play it straight back on the piano.

Budds Farm
31 August

Dearest L,

We enjoyed having you to stay and hope you will come here again before long. I foolishly went to sleep in the sun last week and got a touch of sunstroke which was singularly unpleasant. The Surtees were meant to come to dinner last night but Mrs S has developed some fearful allergy and has a hideous rash from head to foot. By the way, I think Nidnod is the worst bridge player I have encountered in all my life – and the most talkative, too. Your mother's dog shows no sign at all of becoming house trained but luckily his messes are not very large compared with Chappie's. He pursued a small girl riding a bicycle but luckily attempts to make a meal of her right leg proved unavailing. The Cringer's leg has healed up where he was shot. Mr Jackson of the Post Office had a fatal heart attack last week. Your mother is not all that well and is going to see a nose and throat specialist when she comes back from Wales. She gets terribly tired these days but of course she is very highly strung. No news of Lupin getting a job yet. He claims to have caught a shark in Devonshire: in the sea, presumably! I hope Nick Gaselee will come to Henry's dinner. Henry will have to help him with his speech if required to do so. In introducing Nick, it might be worth mentioning that he is a successful trainer of jumpers and has had good winners on the flat as well. He was one of the best amateur riders of his day and has ridden in the Grand National. At one time he was on the racing staff of the Evening Standard and he has also had experience as assistant clerk of the course at Ascot. Mrs Mayhew-Saunders came to lunch yesterday. She is just back from Corfu. Her 14 year old son went snorkelling (is that how you spell it?) and strayed into the area where the nudists bathe. He was rather surprised to see through his mask a nude couple having a stand up go in the water!

Best love from all of us to all of you,

D

P.S. Thank you for your letter.

My father was not keen on Chappie, my dog. I had inherited him from a work colleague and he had never been properly house-trained. He would leave smelly turds in very unfortunate places (Chappie, that is, not my dad). However, my parents' dogs made Chappie look like a saint.

Budds Farm
18 September

Dearest L,

I hope you're all thriving and that Chappie and Henry are both behaving with reasonable decorum. I enclose £5: please get Rebecca something for her birthday. Your mother is in very good form. On Sunday we went to a champagne party with the Cottrills in the morning and to drinks and supper with Aunt Pam and Uncle Ken in the evening. We have killed the geese and the Bomers are coming to help eat one this evening. Mrs Alexander is back home after a nasty operation. The Bomers' old dog Dor died suddenly and I think they all miss her. Your mother's dog is settling down but still makes a fair number of messes. I have not seen Lupin lately and have no idea what he is doing or whether he has any sort of employment. Your mother is off to the funeral of Mrs Tweed who did portraits of you, your brother and your sister in your nursery days. We went to lunch with the Tollers and saw Celia and her baby, a large robust boy like a wrestler. I have sent you 20 polyanthus for your garden from Lowland Nurseries Ltd. They like moist peaty ground and a bit of shade.

Best love,

D

My mother's geese were not a huge success and my father told Lupin that they tasted like a moist flannel shirt.

Budds Farm
12 October

Dearest L,

Your Mother's big luncheon party went off reasonably well. One of the acceptors injured her leg badly in a fall and could not come, and Nidnod's old boy-friend Gervase

O'Donohue died the day before, of old age I presume. The food was excellent and the drink made up for poor quality by being in ample supply. The Burnaby-Atkins had returned from Brazil the day before where they had had a very good time. Hotels, food etc were excellent but the loos less so. You are not permitted to flush paper down the pan but have to put it in a special receptacle where it remains till a slave removes it. The mind boggles! Everyone seemed to enjoy the party but one or two husbands got ticked off by their wives for drinking too much or pinching the wrong bottom. We went to Ascot the day before and had a good lunch with the Abergavennys. I had to judge the horses in one race and the sponsors, Bovis Ltd, gave me a huge bottle of port that I could hardly carry to the car. I think Bovis are builders: I had thought it might be a form of food comprised of Hovis bread and Bovril. Lupin was down here with his friend Elizabeth who I like a lot. Unlike so many of her generation you can carry on a conversation with her without having to spell everything out. In addition she has a well developed sense of the absurd. Not particularly good-looking, but nice hair and excellent legs.

I dread Christmas. I would like to opt out of the so called 'Festive season' and retire to a Jewish hotel in Margate.

Love to all, D x

My father continues to enjoy the company of intelligent young women, especially if they have a good sense of humour and can give as good as they get.

Budds Farm
27 October

Dearest Lumpy,

    I hope you are all reasonably well and behaving with suitable decorum. Life is fairly quiet here with large bills arriving with disheartening regularity. On Saturday we went out to Inkpen and arrived punctually despite Nidnod losing the way. We had been asked for 7.45 but dinner was not until 9.15 p.m. by which time I had drunk a large number of cocktails. I cannot for the life of me recollect what we ate for dinner or what part, if any, I played in the conversation. I do not think my host and hostess were desperately sorry when I eventually took my leave, implanting a kiss on a young girl I claimed to be a newly-found relation. Nidnod lost the way on the journey home. The following day we went to a stand-up lunch at the Parkinsons to celebrate his 60th birthday. Mr P. was in v good form as an aunt aged 94 had kicked the bucket, leaving him a house and some treacle. We arrived at 12:45 but the warm groceries did not materialize till 2.30 p.m. as Mrs P and her mother had had a tiff in the kitchen. Needless to say the guests were all slosherino and not making all that much sense. All this had a bad affect on your mother who was very tiresome when we got home and had a slanging match with a man who had come to stay. I have been buying a book for Mrs Surtees birthday. I chose Porky Pig's Adventures in a Balloon (illustrated). We survived having Aunt Boo to stay though after 48hrs I was on the verge of crowning her with what the police call a blunt instrument. She lives in a fantasy world and never stops talking complete and utter balls. She even out talks your mother, no mean achievement.

Best love to all,

D

The Cringer has just been v sick. I have ordered a new carpet of revolting colour for my bedroom, your mother is installing a bidet in her bathroom. No more news.

Aunt Boo was my mother's highly eccentric sister. My father once said her first husband, who was an actor and often played the part of drunken men, had spent his whole life rehearsing the part.

1980

Chateau Geriatrica
Burghclere

Dearest L,

I hope you are all thriving and that you yourself are conducting your life with appropriate decorum. I saw Loopy at Sandown looking rather damp, cold and dispirited. I went up to London twice last week. The first occasion was a huge lunch at Grosvenor House full of politicians of all parties, trade union leaders, bookmakers, foreign ambassadors and all sorts of riffraff out for a free tuck-in. Just my luck that I found myself seated next to a Newbury neighbour (v rich) with whom I have nothing in common. Two days later I had lunch at the Greenjackets Club with Noel Thistlethwayte and John Surtees. This was good fun though I drank too much and could not keep awake on the journey home. Your mother is in fair form: she has been in Leicestershire with her aunt who is, alas, showing ominous signs of wear and tear. Your mother's dog was slightly seedy after an injection the other day and was fussed over as if it was a delicate baby ten days old. I think the vet must have got a bit browned off! We had a very good dinner with the Surtees on Saturday: a bearded man staying with them for a day knocked off a bottle of whisky and a bottle of gin during the time he was there. I did not take to him all that much. A man was murdered in Newbury on Friday: I did not actually know him but I think he was a tramp who operated a lot in this area. There is a theory he had a quarrel with another tramp when both were sloshed. Lupin is staying with Robin Grant-Sturgis, one of his few friends that so far has managed to keep out of gaol. I had a letter from your godfather Mr Langton-May: he seems to be getting over his heart attack. The weather has been cold and wet and there is no sign of a daffodil yet. The wood stove has been a success and I find if I stoke it up well at bed time it is still going strong at 9 a.m. the next day. Aunt Pam was at Sandown wearing a peculiar hat. The house next to the Alexanders is up for sale, I only hope the purchasers are not as boring as the present occupiers. I had my best jersey cleaned at great expense and within five minutes of putting it on had spilt doughnut jam all down the front. Maddening!

Best love to all,

RM

V. dull letter but news in short supply.

My father once told me that if he was reincarnated he would like to come back as one of my mother's dogs.

Dearest L,

I hope you are all well and flourishing. Jane and Piers have just left. Jane was in good form but looked distinctly tired and seems busy.

When I drove her to the station she found she had no money and touched me for a tenner. Goodbyee ten quid!

Nidnod is much the same as ever but managed to get bitten by Moppet with whose private life she was interfering. I had a letter from Lupin today. It was a catalogue of minor disasters and uncomfortable encounters with weird animals. He rated Nairobi a second class Camberley. He has adopted a toad and named it after Patrick Fisher. I have a severe cold in the head which makes me morose (more so than usual). I took Jane to the Bladon Art Gallery yesterday. She addressed me as 'old Frump' and the lady who runs the gallery thought Jane was referring to her and took umbrage! I bought some fudge there which tasted like a very old cowpat. Cringer very wisely would not touch it. A woman at Newbury has strangled her 82 year old husband with a dressing gown cord. She said he made too many sexual demands but of course she was really after the poor old wreck's money. William Bomer has won a prize at Bradfield for an essay on Oscar Wilde. Not bad at 14!

Best love,

RM xx

P.S. I seem to have got involved in helping to run some racing competition for the 'TV Times' with Brough Scott. I have also let myself in for a BBC radio programme with John Oaksey. My new book 'Derby 200' is due out any time now. I have just read a flattering review of it in some paper. On April 4 we have been asked to the opening of an exhibition of Derby pictures and relics at the Royal Academy. I must make sure I have a clean collar.

Always a mine of information about all sorts of things, local murders in particular.

Chez Nidnod

Dearest L,

Here we are just back from Wales, land of male voice choirs, non-stop rain and ladies with dark moustaches. The weather was perfect when we drove up and perfect when we drove back but it rained without pause when we were there. The country is beautiful and made Scotland look like something on the southern railway about eighteen miles from Waterloo. The hotel was excellent, very comfortable, good service and rich food. The rest did Nidnod good though she slept very badly. The dogs had a marvellous time and loved the huge empty beaches. Solomon is now known as Canute because of his absurd conduct in respect of the sea. I hear Jane has been unwell at the seaside. I expect she has been tucking in unwisely to prawns, crabs etc. I have no idea where Lupin is. I have an idea he may have got bored with those dreary old German lorries he was endeavouring to flog. Your mother has been doing some rather odd microwave cooking including a toad-in-the-hole that gave the impression of having undergone a thorough going over at the local crematorium. We have a fair amount of fruit here and I must start picking blackberries. The Burghclere Barbecue and Firework Display was a success and 2000 people attended. The Lambourn Lurcher Show was good fun too though most of the dogs would be better employed as doormats.

Best love to you all

D

My mother was addicted to buying all the latest gadgets for the kitchen. She bought a microwave literally the second it came on the market. We all groaned when we saw it as we knew what the result would be. Terrible food boiling in the middle and stone cold on the outside. However, she was thrilled when she won a competition held by the manufacturers with the poem, 'Ode to a Microwave'. I can only remember the last line: 'the marvel of a scientist's eye run by electriciteye'. My brother claims my mother's misinterpretation of poetry successfully put him off it for the rest of his life.

1981

Budds Farm
26 April

Dearest Miss Plumpling,

I'm sorry to hear you are not feeling all that well. Try and rest as much as possible. I went to Newmarket last week and the cold was intense. A fat man in a sheepskin coat dropped dead just in front of me. I hear you are off to stay with your sister in Northumberland. If you take that mobile doormat you choose to call a dog, remember that Miss C. is not a dog-lover and that her cat, besides squinting, is very highly strung. I have just bought my summer outfit at Marks and Spencers: i.e. a blue wool and canvas jacket slightly too small, and a pair of shoes (£5) that will disintegrate for sure if they ever get damp. We had a dullish lunch-party last Sunday: a middle-aged lady who had bicycled across America, a man with a beard and another with a speech impediment. The wine I had bought was just short of nasty but they lapped it up and politely suppressed wry grimaces. Lupin has just turned up here; he looks comparatively healthy. Newbury is more tolerable now they have banned cars from the main street. Your mother is seeing an oculist; perhaps the one with slight halitosis who puts his hand on ladies' thighs. Moppet has just brought a decapitated mouse into the kitchen.

Best love

D

My father should never have been allowed to purchase clothing without strict supervision.

Budds Farm
1 July

Dearest Lumpy,

Not much news from here. July has started and I am still in my winter clothes. We did however have a fine evening on Monday so decided to go for a picnic. No expense was spared and your mother opened a tin of Libby's corned beef. Unfortunately she cut her thumb very badly on the tin and I had to drive her to Newbury Hospital where seven stitches were inserted. End of picnic! As a matter of fact the corned beef was not all that good. Last Friday I arranged to meet your scatty sister Jane at 11.45 at an art gallery in Duke Street. I arrived on the tick; no sign of Jane, who turned up 30 minutes late having gone to the wrong Duke Street! It was difficult to see the pictures as the gallery was narrow and the viewers kept on getting in each other's way. We had lunch at a place called the Lafayette. Two watery cocktails (tasted like orange Kia-Ora and ice, nothing else) cost me £6. For lunch we both had sardines in mustard sauce, some boring chicken, raspberries and a bottle of white wine. The bill was £35. Coming out of the restaurant we met Jane's godfather Peter Black, just back from America, and we walked with him to Hatchards where I bought Jane a book. I couldn't get a taxi to Waterloo and the underground was crammed with belligerent adolescents and Germans reading street-maps. I caught a very crowded commuter train to Basingstoke, and between Surbiton and Brookwood a man with really appalling dandruff slept with his head on my shoulder. I was glad to get home to fish-fingers and early bed. Your mother was in Gloucestershire watching polo. We went to a splendid golden wedding lunch party given by Gar and Nancy Barker. A sit-down spread (excellent lobster) for a hundred, lots to drink and admirable service. Gar's speech was not an outstanding success as he quite forgot to mention his wife (the mainstay of the household) and was just sitting down when his daughter shouted out 'What about Mum?' We gave them rather a good book on dogs with many illustrations. I saw Loopy on TV. Old men often do stupid things (don't I know it) and I don't think Loopy was wise to get involved with the SS even though some of them purported to have blue blood and enjoyed hunting and shooting (chiefly Jews).

Have a nice time in Scotland,

XXX R

Loopy (aka Lt-Col Sir George Kennard, my father-in-law) had a very different view on the SS to my father. Richard

Schulze-Kossens, who had been a member of Hitler's personal bodyguard regiment, became friendly with Loopy for a period of time. Loopy, in a moment of comradeship (or madness) invited Richard to his annual regimental dinner and to the Cavalry Memorial Parade in Hyde Park. It was nothing more than a miracle that either or both were not taken outside and shot before the first course.

Budds Farm
12 July

Dearest L,

I hope you had a good time in Scotland. Take as many holidays as you can when you are young: they are apt to be sad affairs when you are old and are really happier pottering about at home and going to bed after the nine o'clock news. Nidnod is in good form but finding her injured thumb painful. Her cooking activities are restricted but she drummed up some rather good macaroni cheese last night. I was at Newmarket last week where it was extremely hot. I drove home during a fearful storm; visibility was almost nil and at one point I found myself going the wrong way round a roundabout. Old Lord Belper asked after you; he is very fat but has not changed much in other directions, I fear! His mother is 88 and in a very bad mood, having lost her driving licence. Patrick, our paper boy, is just off to Scotland (perhaps you'll meet him) for three weeks; he usually goes abroad but he had a fortnight in Spain at Easter! Cousin Tom is trying to persuade me to go to Bali (look it up on the map) in March but I think I am too ancient to disport myself amid all those dusky beauties. Cousin Tom drove his car into a tree last week. The car was wrecked but he was only shaken. The dentist had put 6 stitches in his mouth and then gave him a painkiller which unfortunately sent him to sleep! I heard a rather funny story about a postman but I think you are too young to hear it. Your mother thought it was in very bad taste. Jane's sons are due here soon; I suppose they'll smash the old place up. If it gets really nasty in London, bring Rebecca down here. I had an impudent bird in my room last night and had great trouble in evicting it. It made three messes and annoyed me quite a lot. Did Loopy get any rude letters after his TV appearance? At any rate he has not been bombed (yet)! I'm making one of my rare visits to London this week in order to lunch with Major Surtees. I expect I shall drink too much and get on the wrong train at Waterloo. The police are expecting riots in Reading where there is a large black population. Personally I think this country is slithering towards bankruptcy and bloody revolution. Nidnod is arming herself for a last-ditch stand.

Love to you all from both of us,

RM

In 1981 the United Kingdom suffered serious riots across many major cities in England, including London. At the time we lived in Fulham and my father was concerned for our safety largely because he thought that Fulham and Brixton were one and the same as they were outside Kensington or Chelsea.

Budds Farm

Dearest Lumpy,

Nidnod meant to have her first day's cubbing on Friday but it was cancelled as the head groom at the Old Berks stables wounded a girl groom with a humane killer and then shot himself dead. He had been with the Old Berks for 25 years and was 30 years older than the girl! It is odd how demon sex is always obtruding into fox-hunting. Good old Weavers Gloom trotted up at Folkestone, winning £1,025 and a silver bowl which I have no intention of cleaning.

Lupin seems to be settling down to his work and was last heard driving a crane at St Albans. Your mother is launching out with a lunch party for 22 on Sunday so, as you can well imagine, King Chaos reigns supreme. The guests tend to be elderly and unexciting (like the host and hostess). The dinner Henry kindly asked me to was quite enjoyable though quite different from what I had anticipated and had about as much to do with the racing as had the Labour party conference at Brighton. The theme I discovered on arrival (no one had previously told me) was the presentation of prizes to men and women who had ridden a large number of point to point winners. (Apparently the dinner is an annual event.) There were several speeches, some very long and one farmer from Dorset surprised the ladies with a lengthy story about a horse that could not stop farting. Nick spoke quite well considering he did not really comprehend the theme of the occasion till he got there. I did not realize that Grand Marnier was just one of several hosts and the only person I met representing Grand Marnier was an agreeable man with a beard and unglamorous wife. I baled out soon after the disco started. Major Surtees and I drove back to Newbury in torrential rain. Before the Reading Exit on the M4 it was painfully clear that as a result of the generous Grand Marnier hospitality we both were in dire need of a pee. On the other hand we had no wish to leave the car, dressed as we were in evening clothes. At one point it looked as if my hat would have to be sacrificed but we managed to hold on (not quite literally). At Newbury I transferred to my own car and with singular folly left my suitcase with Major Surtees. I did though, remember to take out 24 bottles of Amontillado. Major Surtees is v pleased as his firm (Garvey's) is now flogging a lot of Sherry to Peter Dominic. Cousin Tom has got a little dog puppy (fawn) called Gilbert, for whom I've fallen in a really big way. Cousin Tom's last remaining aunt, Lady Laurie, died a couple of weeks short of her 100th birthday. She had been dead keen to make her century. My Great Uncle Percy reached 97 and was pinching the bottoms of you girls up till the last. He claimed to have been flogged at Eton the same day as the Battle of Balaclava.

Rebecca seems to be having a good time: I always loathed parties as a child and indulged in a bit of quiet nose-picking combined with a sulk. Not attractive. If I tried to be amusing I always got punished for 'showing off'.

Best love to you all from myself and from Nidnod, D
P.S. Saw Aunt Pam at Newbury races in a hat she must have bought at NAAFI about 35 years ago. No news of Aunt Boo.

Lupin is now operating a crane in a scrap metal yard and my father just manages to avoid using his best trilby as a po.

1982

Budds Farm
1 January

Dearest L,

Happy New Year! Christmas went off very well, you may be slightly surprised to hear! We did not decide to undertake the trip to Northumberland until Christmas Eve as the roads had been in such a ghastly condition but in fact we had a perfectly easy journey. Jane's house was beautifully warm and the food was all that could be desired. When the boys got too rumbustious, I retired to the drawing room where there was a huge fire and masses of books. Nidnod was in her best form and Jane is very good with her. Lupin was there too and consumed a great deal of port. We drove home in exactly six hours despite a good deal of fog. The Cringer was quite happy in his kennel and returned home fat and distinctly smelly. Your mother gave me some winter pyjamas for Christmas and I gave her some glasses for Irish Coffee. I went to the new

Newbury oculist yesterday: he comes from Newcastle and is rather amusing. I hope he knows his job as he has ordered me some new and peculiar spectacles. Peregrine got on well with Paul's Labrador but was once nearly devoured by the Siamese cat. We are having a turkey lunch here on Sunday and the Parkinsons are coming to partake of it. We do have original guests! We are off to play bridge with the Surtees tonight. At least we are sure of a good dinner.

Best love to you all,

D

P.S. We celebrated the New Year here with a lot of smoked salmon and a bottle of good hock. Bed 10 a.m.

From a very early age I had a serious crush on my dad's best friend, Desmond Parkinson, a section head of the secret service. He was a delight to be around – empathetic, complimentary and highly accomplished on the clarinet – and had a number of delightful wives.

Budds Farm
21 January

Dearest L,

We had a terrific storm here last night but most of the roof is still on. Emma LR has been here since Friday and I am happy to say has not changed much! We had a lunch party on Sunday and Emma certainly produced an excellent lunch. Your mother is in very poor form and she and Lupin get on each other's nerves, almost entirely your mother's fault as she will nag and aggravate him when he comes home tired at about 8 p.m. each evening. The Randalls ate some bad fish: Mr Randall came out in a ferocious rash, while Mrs Randall's head swelled to twice its already generous size. Jane seems to be settling down well in her new house. I have not heard of her using her new gun much: at least I have not read about anyone being shot near Corbridge. I have luckily remembered my old Nanny's birthday: I think she is 88 on Friday and still completely on the ball. There are new people in the post office at Burghclere, rather more agreeable than their predecessors but fairly clueless about their work. Your mother has been unable to hunt lately and that makes her somewhat irritable. Her dog is liable to wake me up in the morning by jumping on my bed and sitting on my face. Luckily he does not smell too badly. We have a lot of rats here and they are eating our potatoes with considerable relish.

Best love to all,

D xx

My father's nanny was more than a mother to him than his own mother ever was. He was extremely fond of her and kept in touch with her until she died.

Budds Farm
3 March

Dearest L,

I hope all goes well with you. Things are reasonably placid here. Your mother complains of feeling poorly but declines to see a doctor, pinning her faith to some female masseuse in the locality. Because she is unwell her temper is somewhat uncertain and I have to mind my Ps and Qs (whatever they are, I'm not quite sure). We had a lunch party on Sunday which went off quite well although the Thistles' car broke down and they never got here. Lupin was here and had some brisk arguments with Nidnod. Mark Bomer leaves for France today to study the wine trade near Avignon. The Cringer is much better and has had no more fits of late. Peregrine condescended to get on my lap yesterday but was very sick when he got there. Thanks awfully! Jane apparently enjoyed herself in Devonshire and then at Bath. I rather like Devonshire but have difficulty in keeping awake there. I went to London on Tuesday for a big lunch at the Hyde Park Hotel. I found myself chatting merrily to the Home Secretary and the former editor of The Times so I was moving rather out of my class. Unfortunately I sat next to Sir Gladwyn Jebb, an arrogant old bore who was once our ambassador in Paris. William Douglas Home made a speech but not a particularly good one. I went home by bus and sat next to an Indian who picked his nose with dogged persistence worthy of a nobler cause. Before my bus left I had several glasses of port at Major Surtees's posh office in Curzon Street. Two days earlier his sherry firm (Garvey's) was taken over by the Spanish socialist government! Major S. retires in January and hopes to buy a cottage near Marlborough. Mr Parkinson's elder daughter is back from China and hopes to find work with the BBC. I now do my shopping in Hungerford where car-parking is no problem and the shops are less plebeian than in Newbury. There is rather a good health shop there kept, inappropriately, by a lady who looks on the point of death. She sells non-fattening marmalade that looks and tastes like yellow photo-paste. Good but expensive. A man I saw in church the other day dropped down dead yesterday. Perhaps he did not pray hard enough.

Love to all,

D

My father was not one of life's great believers.

Budds Farm
14 March

Dearest L,

We are off to Glos today to stay with Mrs Pope for Cheltenham. Nidnod is not at all well, bronchitis and diarrhoea. She spent yesterday jump-judging at Tweseldown which probably did not help. Her co-judge was on the verge of a nervous breakdown, something from which her son and daughter are both suffering. Her husband shot himself. Not much news here. 70,000 women demonstrators are expected down here for Easter. There being no loos at Greenham, they leave the Common in a sordid mess. Mrs Surtees is running a takeaway food business; quite good but not exactly cheap. Major S hopes to buy a cottage in Wiltshire. In London last week I drove off in my car, absentmindedly leaving my overcoat on the roof. It went into orbit passing The Ritz and I was lucky to get it back! The Cringer is well but incontinent. A man came to repair my arm chair; he said it would cost over £200 so I told him to go away. Nick Gaselee's horse

Keengaddy won at Sandown on Saturday and it must have a chance in the Grand National. Mr Randall managed to pull down a shelf in my bathroom, breaking various items. I saw Aunt Pam at Sandown; she did not look too good. Uncle Ken's nose is entirely covered with white hair.

Love to all,

D

Uncle Ken was inflicted not only by a lot of white hair on his nose but also coming out his ears, hence the nickname my daughter gave him: Uncle Whiskers. His wife (Lady D aka The Hamburger) was on the bossy side, like an instructor at the pony club.

The Crumblings
Monday

Dearest Lumpy,

I trust you are all thriving. Lupin stayed here last night. He hopes to drive a juggernaut to Poland this week but as he has no visa I regard him as a non-starter. Your mother enjoyed her trip up to the Tordays'. Jane's cat sprang on Peregrine and started to eat him but Peregrine's yells of protest and terror luckily brought his outraged owner to his rescue. Weaver's Loom was second in a £10,000 race at Cheltenham and thereby earned £2,110 which is better than a poke in the eye with a sharp stick. Cousin Tom got mugged in South Audley Street. A man sloshed him on the skull with a length of lead piping and then removed his wallet etc. Tom came round in Middlesex Hospital where he was sewn up, looking a sorry sight. He has to rest at home for 3 weeks. He has taken it very well but after all he is seventy! The garden is very dry and full of dead shrubs killed by the January weather. I saw Aunt Pam at Cheltenham: her breathing is none too good. My old Nanny, Mabel, now aged ninety, sent me a lively post-card from Sturminster Newton where she has been on holiday. She paid a visit to Marnhull. Tell Charlotte B the bathing season will be opening soon. Will she give me a swimming lesson for a small fee?

Love to you all from all of us here

XX D

My brother Lupin sets off driving an articulated lorry full of medical supplies for Poland with his new and highly unlikely friend, Molly the Marchioness of Salisbury, as his navigator. Astonishingly, in order to raise money for their Polish adventure they threw a ball at Hatfield House with Prince Charles and Princess Diana as guests of honour. My brother told me I was going to sit next to a building society manager from Wolverhampton, who in reality turned out to be Spike Milligan.

The Crumblings
Burghclere
6 April

Dearest L,

I hope you are behaving yourself reasonably well. Has Henry been conscripted into the Army yet? I expect he will be. With his knowledge of liquid refreshment, I expect he will be put into the Army Catering Corps. In 1945 I was sent on a commanding officers' cooking course at Aldershot. One of my instructors was the head baker from Lyons, another a chef from the Savoy. In the POW camp I was for a year Mess Cook with Peter Black. Our speciality was bread and potato pie, alternated with a pudding made from crushed biscuit crumbs and dried figs (v good for bowels). Your mother is in belligerent form. We are having the conservatory done up. The result is that it looks like a moderately clean lavatory at a provincial railway station. Deepest Gloom was beaten by a neck in a £2,000 race last week. However he has won over £3,000 in win and place money this season which eases the pain somewhat. The Hislops are just back from Provence. They boarded a French plane but a strike was called and they had to get off. They were just transferring to an Italian plane when the crew walked off over some grievance. They then started off in a car but the motorways were blocked by striking lorry-drivers. Eventually they boarded a boat at Dieppe. There were 250 London schoolchildren on board, 247 of which were extremely sick. The Cringer is very well and getting rather fat. The Post Office has obtained a licence to sell drink. (Big opportunity for Henry, perhaps?)

Best love to you all,

D

Much to everyone's horror we are now at war and our troops have been sent to the Falklands. My father can't resist the opportunity to have a dig at Henry who years earlier had managed to fail his officer's exam and thus failed to get a commission in the army.

Budds Farm
24 August

Dearest L,

V cold and grey here, more like early March. Your mother is off to London to see Aunt Boo who has bronchitis and is fairly groggy. I have heard nothing from Jane lately: I believe Lupin is off to Germany. We had a good dinner at La Riviera last night: only £40 for four, cheap by the hideous standards of today. Solomon is very tiresome as about seven local bitches are on heat. Newbury Carnival took place yesterday and the streets are even dirtier than usual. Mr Thorn was nearly electrocuted when doing some repairs on Friday. The electrician had told him a cable was dead when in fact it was very lively indeed. Four Fishers came to lunch on Friday: Mrs F now drives a jumbo-sized Mercedes. Marcus Fisher killed 2 pheasants, thereby anticipating the start of the season by a couple of months. We ourselves are going to Wales for a few days, somewhere near Harlech. I rather like the Welsh, they are amusingly sly and dishonest. As a matter of fact I tend to get on well with most foreigners bar the Scotch whom I dislike quite a lot. I loathe bagpipes, kilts, the Scottish accent and the barbaric cooking at Scotch hotels. Argyllshire reminded me of Woking except that the ponds were bigger and the food far worse. I rather like Belgium – hideous, quarrelsome people but excellent cooks and gardeners. I also rather like Egyptians who are too idle even to flick away the bluebottles crawling over their eyeballs. I don't know Poland very well but lived there for a bit. Most Poles are romantic but agreeable. I think I can still say 'Good

Morning' and 'This lavatory smells awful' in Polish. My Arabic is limited to 'Does your father live in the Old City?' Not very useful, on the whole! I rather think the Arabic for 'Impossible' is 'mushmumkin'. It was unfortunate that the Arabic for 'Allied Military Government' was the same as for 'dog-turd'.

Love to all,
XX D

Dinner at La Riviera is one of the highlights of my father's life, but he is not as enthusiastic about either Scotland or its inhabitants.

Chez Nidnod
Monday

Dearest L,

I hope you had a nice time in sunny Devonshire and that you behaved with reasonable decorum. Nidnod is in very good form, Peregrine having been declared 'Champion dog' at the Flower and Dog show. I had hoped the Cringer would win the Veterans Class but he was in a bad mood and refused to co-operate. However he was placed second despite peeing on the judge's handbag. There were some good stalls at the show and I bought a plum cake for £1 and 2 books for 5p each. I did a very good vase (red dahlias and carnations with grey foliage) for the Floral Decoration Class but had no luck; the prize went to some frightfully chi-chi exhibit, old man's beard and stinkwort in what looked like an old shoe. I went to a rather ghastly funeral last week, the climax came when a royal Artillery Trumpeter played the Last Post while the organist was flat out with Sheep May Safely Graze. Lupin is here (plus dog) and has gone to see some quack over near Basingstoke. All men are hypochondriacs at heart. We have 20 people coming to lunch on Sunday and already Nidnod is rather excited. I am getting in lots of Spanish brandy of the kind that would make a week old corpse leap lightly from the coffin and enter for a six day race. My watch has gone wrong for the first time since I bought it in Hartley Wintney five years before you were born. (Not very interesting but I'm pushed for news.)

Best Love and a XXX for Rebecca

D

Flower arranging is not a skill one would immediately associate with my father. However, he could actually put together quite a good display.

Budds Farm
5 September

Dearest L,

Not many squeaks from you lately! Nidnod is well but worried because old Doris Bean, who keeps her horse and is 81, fell down in her kitchen last week and broke her thigh. No joke at that age – or at any other age, either! I took Nidnod and the dogs for a walk by the River Kennett the other afternoon. When we got home panting for a cup of tea Nidnod discovered she had dropped the burglar-alarm keys so we were locked out. We had to drive back to where we had walked, and thanks to my Boy Scout training the keys were found! Mrs Surtees took Peregrine's mother to the West Ilsley Dog Show. The poor little thing (the dog, not Mrs S.) was attacked by a lurcher who was dragged off just in time. Seven stitches had to be inserted at a cost of £35.

I suppose I had a couple of pleasant days at Brighton staying with Cousin John in his flat overlooking the nudist beach. My accountant has had 2 heart attacks and his stand-in annoys me beyond belief. I think I shall give him the tin-tack. We attended the opening of the Drag Hunt's new Kennels near Lambourn. The Master saw fit to make a speech containing three exceptionally vulgar stories which shocked the adults but were greeted with howls of delight by the many children present. Mrs Surtees came to lunch in the garden last week and I provided a delicious hock cup. Nidnod and Mrs S both felt very poorly afterwards and I think I must have overdone the 'special offer' Bulgarian brandy. I had quite a bad headache myself. No news of your brother who, as far as I know, and I don't know much, is still unemployed. Mrs Gaselee is recovering slowly from a fractured skull. We did not go to the Lambourn Lurcher Show yesterday: too many gypsies and thieves of every description.

Best love,

D

My father's letters were better than any gossip column and probably more accurate.

Budds Farm
Monday

Dearest L,

So sorry to learn that Rebecca's godfather and your great friend had died. I assume not unexpectedly. It is sad when some old buffer who has been a friend of mine for years drops off the hook: it is infinitely worse when a young man in his prime is the victim.

All my sympathy to you and Henry.

D

Andy Loch was – and still is – sadly missed. At his memorial service half the congregation was made up of crying girls!

Home of Rest for Impoverished Members of the Middle Class
Burghclere
11 October

Dearest L,

I hope all goes well with you. Plenty of rain here and the garden very muddy in consequence. Nowadays Mr Randall turns up in very posh clothes, attired for a luncheon party in SW1 rather than for digging manure into the vegetable plot. This week-end he and Mrs R are off on a coach tour in Devonshire. They have a much better time than Nidnod and I do. It has been truly said that the pleasures of youth are not really pleasures, and that the consolations of old age do not exist at all. Jane is glowing with pride after her article in the 'Daily Telegraph'. I worked for the DT for eight weeks in 1955. The Sports Editor was always sloshed by teatime and I had the utmost difficulty in getting paid. We went out to dinner with some very nice people last Wednesday, rich too, but the repast was revolting. The first course looked and tasted like Sunlight Soap. I sat next to a fearsome old bag, Lady Grimthorpe, who feigned deafness. In my view she is an absolutely ideal candidate for the lethal chamber. The following day we had a very good lunch with John Abergavenny who is giving up his job as the Queen's Ascot Representative. I think Nidnod was sitting next to a trainer who has become a millionaire by shrewd property deals. Most of his horses belong to an Arab who runs a series of highly profitable abortion clinics in Hammersmith. I was introduced to a v small Polish girl whom I thought was having a day off from a local school. However later I saw her with her noggin in a tankard of the hard stuff and discovered she was 26! Poor old Solomon is getting very frail and simply could not jump up on my bed this morning. His appetite, though, remains unimpaired.

Did you hear about the lady who had three whippets? She called them 'whippetin, whippetout and whipe-pet'.

I hate my new accountant who looks like Himmler and is liable to behave like him, too. Mrs Hislop recently met

Loopy's first wife, I think her name is Cecilia, and said she was very good looking still. Someone I met, possibly Emma's brother, mucks in with Henry's brother at Bristol Univ. I hear the glamorous Miss Blacker is being courted by an individual called 'John the Barman'.

Best love,

D

Did you know that Harry Randall is rhyming slang for candle?

My father is equally unimpressed with the Daily Telegraph, Lady Grimthorpe and his new accountants.

1983

Budds Farm
9 February

Dearest L,

V many thanks for your well-chosen card. You should have seen some of the night nurses at Basingstoke! They were capable of anything. I am now back to normal, not that that really amounts to much. Nidnod is somewhat overwrought and better before 6 p.m. than after. She simply refuses to relax and cannot understand why she is always tired. I am thinking of writing an adventure story for small children called 'The Desperate Adventures of Peregrine, the Dog Detective'. The Cringer is well, but apt to regard the interior of Budds Farm as his personal lavatory. Mr Randall is just off to Leeds to bury his brother-in-law. Aunt Joan's greatest friend, Marjorie Napier, was found dead in her bath, presumably after a heart attack. She had been there quite a long time. That sort of thing is the fate that elderly people living alone all dread. The Greenham Common women are becoming rather a bore: a pack of savage, men-hating left-wing lesbians! I have just been invited to a champagne and oysters party in London at Bentleys. I certainly propose to accept. We have been invited to meet the Queen M at lunch on Friday. I must make sure I have a clean collar. Lupin seems in good form and seems to think he is the young tycoon of N.W. Kensington & District.

Best love to all

D

Unsurprisingly my father and other locals clearly had disparaging views of the Greenham Common Women's Peace Camp, which had been going strong since September 1981.

Budds Farm
22 February

Dearest L,

Was it you who sent me rather a pert Valentine card? I thought I recognised your writing but could not be sure! V cold here and I am wearing as many clothes as I did in Poland in 1941. Your mother is in poorish form and seems to take a dim view about everyone (bar Paul) and everything (bar the Old Berks Hunt)! Sometimes her views are so violent that I think she will attack the Greenham Common women, for example. I wish you could cheer her up a bit. We are having a lunch party on Sunday but unfortunately her rich boy-friend Rodney Carrott will be in Kenya. Perhaps he will meet up with Aunt Pam! Solomon is much better now that we have stopped giving him pills: I think vets are as dangerous with pills as doctors are. I made rather a good drink the other day: 1/3rd Spanish brandy, 1/3rd white rum and 1/3rd cointreau. The guests were quite chatty afterwards and your mother never drew breath for a second. Your mother is furious with Mrs Block who made critical comments about Peregrine's domestic and sexual habits. She will never be forgiven. The Bomers are building an additional garage and the lane has been blocked with bulldozers, gravel lorries etc. I have heard nothing from Jane recently; she is more long-winded on the telephone than anyone I've ever met. How is Rebecca? I suppose it is a slack time of the year for children's parties. An army of moles is rapidly destroying my lawn and I have been singularly unsuccessful in killing any. A golden pheasant is busy removing the buds off my polyanthi. I have got to attend a boring lunch at the Hyde Park Hotel next week. I think I'll go up by bus.

Love to you all at Clancarty Road,

D xx

Best of British Luck with your driving test.

Depressingly I fail my driving test for the sixth time.

Budds Farm
1 April

Dearest L,

Happy Easter to you wherever you are: I assume in
Devonshire. V cold here and I can't get going in the garden
which continues to be in a sad condition. Two funerals last
week, one at Windsor and the other at East Woodhay. The
Cringer is well and managed to open Nidnod's handbag and
remove a large bar of milk chocolate. Nidnod has back trouble,
bronchitis and diarrhoea, which happen to be about the only
3 diseases I have not got at present. She makes matters worse
by refusing to give up hunting, and long hours in a biting east
wind are hardly calculated to relieve her situation. All in all,
she is in very poor form. The Newbury area has been invaded
by hordes of savage women, not one of whom could truthfully
be called a sex object. They look more like Feldwebels from
the SS. Major Surtees went to see a quack about his arthritic
knee and was charged 65 guineas for a consultation! I went to
Basingstoke Hospital for a check-up and was seen by a man
who looked like an Indian jockey. He said I was more or less
OK and should be able to struggle on for a bit, doubtless to the
irritation and disappointment of some of my near-and-dears!
We have got a lot of Nidnod's relatives to lunch on Sunday
and Nidnod is producing a turkey. I am mixing a little cocktail
called 'Between The Sheets' which contains almost everything
bar gin. The Bomers are all away for Easter, I think down on
the coast of Kent where the east wind should be reasonably
keen. Nidnod is working on the Tote at the local point-to-point
on Monday. I have just had some curious gravel for breakfast

called 'Grapenuts'. We used to be given it on Sundays at my preparatory school in place of porridge. I have not heard much from Jane lately: I believe it is Piers's birthday on April 6. I haven't seen Rebecca for ages. Has she grown much?

Best love to all,

D

One of my dad's most thumbed books, Black's Comprehensive Medical Dictionary, 1879 edition, was kept in the downstairs loo. He would consult it regularly and then convince himself he had the most unpleasant diseases.

Budds Farm
22 April

Dearest L,

Thank you for your letter. These big offers are of course very tempting. I think Henry ought to consult a top class solicitor (not some moth-eaten old dodderer in Tiverton) or at any rate his bank manager provided the branch of the bank is a big London one and not some two-man affair that opens from 11 a.m. to 1 p.m. on Tuesdays and Fridays. I myself always feel inclined to play safe in matters like this but of course there are people who take an entirely different viewpoint and quite often they are highly successful. Cousin Tom is the only member of my family competent to advise but he is convalescent after a ghastly operation for a brain tumour and is at present in no condition to advise Henry or anyone else. Have you thought of having a talk with your godfather Frank Byrne? He is quite shrewd.

I'm glad to hear you like your house in the country. Do please ask your mother and me down to see it one afternoon during the summer.

I am not surprised to hear that Rebecca is considered intelligent. Don't be bullied by her headmistress. You are probably the best judge of what Rebecca needs. I have not been very well lately. I collapsed when clearing some undergrowth but just managed to stagger to the house where Nidnod found me unconscious on the kitchen floor. Dr Keeble said I had had a stroke, but Dr Taylor disagreed and now Dr K has come round to her point of view. I feel pretty ghastly but have no alternative but to carry on as before. If Nidnod or I stop, the place goes to pot. It is really too big for a couple of oldies and I would like to move but Nidnod is anything but keen. When I cool, which may not be very far off now, I think she will move out of this area altogether. I find old age increasingly bloody. Most of my friends are dead, undergoing major surgery or are confined in private asylums near Bognor Regis. I seem to have no purpose in life and irritate your mother considerably with the result that my emergence from the doghouse is a rarity. I hope you'll come down here and see me before I give the bucket a resounding kick.

We are due to fly to Crete on May 9 but I am very shaky and your mother is in very poor form too so it'll be a miracle if we both get there and both get back!

Love to you all, and my very best love to you, my dearest L.

D xx

My father was not an easy patient when he was ill. He would frequently resort to emotional blackmail as well as offering Beckie rich prizes in the hope that we would jump on a train to Newbury in order to nurse and entertain him, which we normally ended up doing.

Budds Farm
25 May

Dearest L,

The holiday was quite a success. V good weather after the first two days. Hotel comfortable, lovely garden. Our chalet within piddling distance of the sea. We had a fridge in our room and often had lunch and cold drinks on our balcony. We also had a sort of immersion heater for making tea, coffee. Hotel food ghastly, looked like dog turds and probably tasted similar. Some good meals though in small seaside tavernas. Local fish called Woppas. Topless German bathers with boobs like overfilled sandbags. Italian ladies who never shave under the arms. In our hotel were Peter Close and Alan Colls from Yateley. Also Rosemary Grissell whom you may have met. Nidnod enjoyed herself and was mostly in good form. Sorry to hear Jane is having to leave her house.

XX D

'Quite a success' is rich praise from my dad after a holiday.

Budds Farm
30 June

Dearest L,

Thank you for your card. You seem to be living it up lately. Quite right, too, at your age. I'm just crawling around an object of no interest to anyone bar undertakers. I'm off to Brighton tomorrow for a bit of sea air with Cousin John. Next week we are off to Shropshire for a couple of nights. I can't think why I agreed to go. Your mother is in quite good form. Unfortunately she has been given some cooking books and is apt to experiment on me. Poor old Cringer is very tottery; his legs gave way this morning and he could not get going again for some time. He and I make a good pair.

Best love,
XX RM

More despondency from Chateau Glum.

Budds Farm
21 August

Dearest L,

I hope you are behaving with reasonable decorum. All v quiet here. Uncle Ken & Aunt Pam stayed the night. Aunt Pam manages to convey the impression that she more or less disapproves of everything. I can't say it bothers me all that much! They are off to Kenya this winter. Major Surtees stayed, too. He is rather poorly with arthritis and is getting ominously lame. Your mother is in good trim and enjoyed a day's sailing with her rich and portly boy-friend Rodney Carrott. She stayed with the Thistlethwaytes at Bembridge and met a lot of old friends. Peregrine was extremely sick yesterday and Solomon piled up a pyramid on the dining-room carpet. I hope they won't make a habit of this sort of thing. We have a plague of magpies here: I think they have seen off the rabbits. Nidnod got a 'Highly Commended' for Flower Decoration at the local Flower Show. Judy Gaselee is recovering rather slowly from a fractured skull. We had a good lunch yesterday with Bobby Kennard and his ever-loving wife. Bobby certainly seems to have landed up on the pig's back. Their most promising horse met with a fatal accident last week. Major Barlow's two year old filly, worth £100,000, broke a leg in a race at Newbury and had to be put down. Weaver's Loom looks plump and healthy and is eating me into insolvency. How is Rebecca? I suppose her summer holiday is nearly over. Lupin is due here tonight. I've no idea what he is doing or how he gets enough money to eat. He and I have been invited to a champagne party at the next Newbury race-meeting. Next week we are going to a Cameron family lunch party at the Café Royal to meet the elder Cameron boy's Swiss fiancée. I find most Swiss excruciatingly dull but they make excellent hotel managers. I was cut dead by Mrs Hislop at Newbury. Hooray!

Best love,

D

Weaver's Loom was one of the racehorses in which my father

had a share with his friends, the Gaselees. He had run well in
some races but not well enough as he became known to us as
'Deepest Gloom'.

Budds Farm
Thursday

Dearest L,

It really was kind of you to have both your aged parents
to stay and to take such trouble to give them a good time.
We are both very grateful. I like Overlands very much indeed
and think it has immense possibilities. You certainly own
what I feel sure must be the most extraordinary bookcase in
this country! I enjoyed the picnic but would not like to walk
over that particular field very often wearing plimsolls. As
for your daughter, she is first-class entertainment and I have
never met a child of that age with such a comprehensive
vocabulary!

Our hotel was very agreeable, an excellent room, large
garden, swimming pool and good food bar a repulsive
pudding erroneously described as 'trifle'. We had a smooth
trip home, the only incident being when we stopped for a
drink and Peregrine was confronted by a Great Dane.

I was terribly sorry to hear about your driving test and
you must have been bitterly disappointed. Don't lose heart:
before your next try, get your London Dr to give you some
of those pills that jockeys take before they ride in the Grand
National. It might do the trick.

With singular senile folly I left some things, plus a nice pen Nidnod gave me, on the mantelpiece. Could you please send them on? I enclose £1 for postage.

Very best love,

D

My parents' visit was a lot more successful than the previous time when we had no running water. My father spent a lot of his stay chilling in a deckchair, a sitting target for my daughter's version of the musical Cats. There was only one drama of note, which was when I took them for a picnic and we ended up in a field that had just been sprayed with liquid manure.

Budds Farm
14 September

Dearest L,

How goes it? Have you had your first autumn cold yet? I believe Rebecca's birthday is next week. I hope I sent you a cheque on her behalf but if I haven't let me know. I'm so forgetful nowadays. Did you enjoy Burghley? It did not look the best of fun on TV. Nidnod is suffering from depression (not uncommon with women of her age) so I am giving her lunch at The Furzebush at East Woodhay. I have been planting out polyanthi, my favourite spring flowers. When you handle them, bear in mind that some people are allergic to them and are liable to come out in cracked hands afterwards. Eight years ago I planted two plum trees. Until this summer not a single plum appeared; this year there is a bumper crop. Locals say my marigolds have attracted the right sort of bee for pollination! On the other hand no apples and pears which usually do well. Aunt Pam is back from Jersey and said the gin was running out of her ears. Some people have all the luck. A local lady of 96 has been killed in a motor accident: her chauffeur was 85. I'm not looking forward to the winter, it really isn't much fun when you are old and living in a chilly house in genteel poverty. The Very Rev Holmes Dudden, Vice-Chancellor, Oxford University, who used to wear a fur coat and smoke chair-leg cigars, once observed, after his third glass of port: 'As an ordained clergyman of the Church of England I am constrained to believe in a future life, but I don't mind admitting, my dear fellow, that personally I should much prefer extinction.' I wonder if your local library has a novel called 'Scandal' by F. B. Wilson? It is mildly amusing. I am sure the next war will be started by some idiot, slightly pissed, pressing the wrong button, causing the entire planet to disintegrate.

Best love to you all from all of us, including Baron Otto,

XX D

Baron Otto, my father's new Chihuahua, brings a little joy into his life but does not stop him imparting his views on both winter and the end of the world.

Budds Farm
25 September

Dearest L,

How are you all? I am glad to hear Rebecca's party went off well. Emma Lemprière-Robin is staying here and cheers us up. She is hunting with the Old Berks this season and will keep Nidnod on her toes in more ways than one! Baron Otto is in good form and gives me a sharp nip every now and then if he is displeased. He and Peregrine are now good friends. We are just off to Virginia Water to meet Sandra Cameron and her Australian husband. He comes from a pretty rough part of that continent and I hope he is not an aboriginal. Nidnod and I went out to dinner with the Airds and played bridge. We both lost: Nidnod seems to think bridge is the same as poker with unfortunate results, not least for her partner! I received an enormous book yesterday compiled by Brough Scott and costing £25. It has some marvellous pictures in it. It is a pity Brough wrote a message for me in it or it would have done for the Darlings Christmas present. Your Aunt Barbara came to lunch here on Thursday; she is as barmy as ever but really doesn't talk more balls than her sisters. Weavers Loom is as lame as Long John Silver and I fear we may have to put him down. We are having a conference on Tuesday. I won 3 bottles on the charity day at Ascot but alas, one held mineral water, the second an unpopular brand of beer and the third sweet martini which makes me feel sick. What really annoyed me was that Michael Philips won a crate of champagne. I am going up to Newmarket on Wednesday to see Cousin Tom who has been told he has cancer. Charlie Blackwell's wife has just left him which does not surprise me. His mother was always leaving people. Aunt Joan is just off to Crete. Recently the electricity failed at the Hotel we stayed at in Crete. Two elderly guests broke legs trying to find their chalets in pitch darkness. Two English girls were raided in their chalet by intoxicated Greek waiters and a young man who came to their aid walked through a glass door and had to be removed in a plain van.

XXXX D

Love to all

My mother was a great games player. She was also very competitive and hated to lose; on occasions she was known to expand the rules in her favour, especially when playing backgammon.

Budds Farm

5 October

Dearest Lumpy,

I am glad to hear the wedding went off well even though Rebecca went a bit berserk at the reception! Your mother has gone off to Somerby to see Mrs Falkner, a long trip in one day. She'll be very tired when she gets back. Kate kindly sent us some photographs. The one of Rebecca was excellent. The one of myself administered a painful shock. I look like a fortnight-old corpse exhumed for examination by the Home Office pathologist. Bobby Kennard sent a yearling up to the Newmarket Sales and got 78,000 guineas for it. Rather a lark in view of the fact that a few years back if overcoats for elephants had been 5p each, he could not have bought a pair of gaiters for a canary. Otto is well and very bouncy. Yesterday we had lunch at the White Hart at Hamstead Marshall with Sarah and Mark Bomer. I thought the fried squid tasted like a very old bicycle tyre. I have just received three books to review, two of them very boring. Peregrine is getting portly: not enough exercise and too much rich food. I see one of the boys tried to blow up Wellington: I imagine he will get the sack. After all, even in these days dynamiting your school is fairly serious. They have always had a lot of criminals at Wellington; when we lived at Yateley a dangerous gang of local burglars was found to be boys at Wellington. One Old Wellingtonian I knew was involved in a notorious jewel robbery at the Hyde Park Hotel. It was very nearly murder and if it had been he would have swung for sure. The Randalls are away in Scotland for a fortnight: they have only just come back from Blackpool. I have my share in Weavers Loom and now have a share in rather a common horse with the odd name of Gay Tent. The Adams boys have both passed in to Oxford, one into Christchurch, the other into Magdalen. Not bad considering that after Horris Hill they went to the state school in Newbury.

Best love to you all from all of us,

D

P.S. Cousin Caroline sent 3 yearlings at Newmarket. There was no bid for either of the first two but the third made 410,000 guineas! Nice work if you can get it!

Clearly cousin Caroline has all the luck.

Budds Farm
26 October

Dearest L,

Thank you for your letter. Yes, do come down on November 20th. If you bring Chappie please prevent him from using the new dining room carpet as a loo. Also, please stop him attacking Emily, my tame hen, who is usually outside the front door hoping for food. She sometimes follows me into the house. I hope Rebecca has fully recovered and I gather she managed to enjoy her birthday party. Nidnod arrived safely at Jane's house and is evidently enjoying herself. We went to the Herns' party on Sunday: mostly stable lads and their girls but the Queen was there too. Otto is in good form but Nidnod spoils him. Luckily he cannot jump up on my bed yet. I have quite a merry time when Nidnod is away as I'm out to lunch and dinner every day. Are you in touch at all with Frank Byrne and his wife? I hear that Lorna had a nasty fall and hurt her arm while Frank has been in Charing Cross Hospital and may have had a mild stroke. Aunt Joan evidently enjoyed her holiday in Crete. We went to the play – The Mikado – done by the local school. The orchestra and the chorus were excellent but none of the principals could sing. One of the boys aged 15 had a beard and looked about 42.

Love to all,

D

Apparently Chappie and Otto justify more comment from my father than hanging out with the Queen.

1984

Budds Farm
26 February

Dearest L,

I hope all goes well with you. I am thankful the winter is
almost over though I rather dread having to start gardening
again which is now beyond my strength. I long to live
somewhere smaller: or perhaps I shall seek refuge in one of
the Newbury geriatric homes if I can find enough money. Otto
is very well and keeps my feet warm at night. A magpie has
just come and raided Emily's nest, pinching three of her eggs.
Your mother blames me for that and thinks I should stand
on permanent sentry duty. Incidentally your mother is in very
bad form and I think finds me an intolerable burden. 'There'll
be no moaning at the bar when I put out to sea.' I went to
a cremation at Slough last week. The parson had forgotten
or mislaid his teeth and I could not tell if he was reciting the
Nicean Creed or giving out the runners for the first race at

Kempton. Not much news in Burghclere, but there never is. It is one of England's most boring villages. 'The Directory of the Turf' (price £30) gives the date of my birth as 1090 and spells Burghclere wrong. We are going to the Canaries for a week in April which I dread. I believe it is a concrete jungle with masses of lower-middle-class Germans. Lupin came to lunch a week ago with an uncouth man and an amusing woman whose hair badly needed combing. They arrived an hour late which did not increase the warmth of their reception. I see from 'The Times' it is dangerous to drink Chianti if you are taking anti-depressant pills. I went to Kempton on Saturday and had lunch with a charming Italian who hated racing. She was very interested in Otto. Anyway she cheered me up temporarily. Life here is about as hilarious as waiting for a train at Basingstoke on a cold February morning. Gay Tent is lame again and I shall get rid of my share in him as soon as I decently can.

Love to all,

D

My father's latest horse, Gay Tent, was not a big success and was nicknamed Homosexual Marquee by Lupin.

Budds Farm
10 May

My Dearest L,

V. cold and grey here and the garden is brown and dry. As no doubt Nidnod told you, our holiday was a disaster of the

first magnitude. The Canaries are a hideous, treeless dump.
We had a bleak sunless room looking out on to concrete. Not
a glimpse of the sea. A troop of randy peacocks screeched
without ceasing all day. Hordes of fat women from Stuttgart
and Düsseldorf sprawled topless round the pool, flaunting
bosoms like half-filled hot-water bottles. I never want to see
a pair of Teutonic tits again. The food was moderate and the
shopping centre slummy. Luckily the Lemprière-Robins were
there to have a laugh with. Nidnod had given me hell for
not booking for a fortnight; when we were there she could
hardly bring herself to stay a week! The flight, both ways,
was long and uncomfortable and I really was thankful to
get home back to income tax demands and a monumental
pile of bills. I have bought a new car (Volkswagen Golf)
to economise on petrol. I discovered quite a nice house at
Kintbury. When I showed it to Nidnod in 'Country Life' she
said nothing would induce her to live in a dump like that
and she refused to look at it. I went on my own, liked it,
and persuaded her to look at it that afternoon. She fell for
it in a big way and is now keener than I am! Lupin liked it
too. Whether our bid will be sufficient remains to be seen.
We saw a house at Hurstbourne Tarrant with a nice garden
but really only suitable for a bachelor who does not mind
discomfort and does not wash much. Nidnod has a bad cold
and is in a very difficult mood. I seem to have a lot of really
boring work on my hands. The Randalls' Golden Wedding
went off well.

Best love to you all,
D

Before moving from Budds Farm to The Miller's House my parents decided they needed to make some cutbacks. One of these cutbacks was to cancel the Daily Mail, which would have been successful if they had not both driven into Newbury every day to buy one.

Budds Farm
Monday

Dearest L,

I suppose after your recent triumph you are driving all over the country in a large motor-car supplied by Henry's company. I expect, though, that before long Henry will buy you a nice little motor of your own. I recommend a Volkswagen Golf. Life here is very unsettled and your poor mother is in a very highly-strung condition. Sometimes she seems quite keen on moving, at others she loathes the new house and everything to do with it. She is particularly controversial after 7 p.m. when she is tired! To make things worse Golly is slightly lame and this misfortune is regarded as of world-shattering importance. I have not seen Lupin since he left that peculiar place at Weston-super-Mare in Somerset: I think it is a sort of loony bin. He has to sleep in a dormitory with other nut-cases. I hope he likes it. I hope the 'cure' did in fact cure him. Of course he is rather restricted being without a car. I met Miss Vallence at a drink party the other day; she has not changed much. I see Tiny Clapham is one of our hopes for the Olympic Games. It has been very hot and dry here but

I'm glad to say we had a few drops of rain this morning. Poor old Lord Carnarvon had a hideous operation in Basingstoke last Wednesday but managed to survive. I think he is 86. Did you see that your mother's friend Sylvia Bowditch had been left £7,000,000 by the old trout she had lived with for the last 20 years? What will a single woman of 71 do with seven million? I go over to The Miller's House most days and try and tidy up the garden. The fig tree there has quite a lot of figs on it but I expect the birds will get most of them. Mrs Cameron has been staying here: she is a calming influence on Nidnod and is also very helpful over the house. Both dogs are well (Henry will be disappointed to hear that) and are yapping a lot and biting the legs of visitors to whom they take a dislike. I hope we have sold Budds Farm but no house is sold till the lolly is safely in the Bank. Jane enjoyed her stay in France; luckily the state of their finances permitted them to go to the most expensive hotel in France (or one of the most expensive). There is a veritable forest of rhubarb at the new house. Perhaps they all suffered from constipation. Mr Parkinson's step-son has suddenly turned up from Hong Kong and wants to live with him. He is dead unlucky over his relations.

Love to all, D xx

Having failed my driving test for the seventh time my brother Lupin gave me a Valium and I passed on the eighth go. Luckily my driving test took place before my brother booked himself into Broadway Lodge, a drug rehabilitation centre. It was not a sort of loony bin, as my father liked to describe it.

Budds Farm
Tuesday

My Dearest L,

I'm so sorry to hear Rebecca is poorly. It must be a
worry for you and I hope the Hospital sorts out the trouble
without delay. She looks a very healthy child so I do not
for a moment imagine anything serious is the matter. In the
meantime, all my sympathy and please give my love to the
patient. I hear Jane has run over a motor-cyclist. How very
careless of her! I fear she may be rather heavily fined. People
are rolling up to look at Budds Farm, most of them very nice.
It is fatiguing showing them round but more so for them as
Nidnod never stops talking, giving the impression that the
property belongs entirely to her and that I am only a lodger.
Yesterday some rather nice people called Du Pree arrived at
7.45 p.m. by which time Nidnod was a bit muddled and I
heard her say that the cellar was usually under water. Later
she was threatening to shoot Jester who had annoyed her
in some way. She gave me a very nice picnic basket as a
present yesterday morning but by the evening decided I was
unworthy of it and she now intends to give it to someone
else. Such is life! This morning a very good-looking merchant
banker is making a second inspection. He is half Peruvian,
half Swedish, is a member of the Turf Club and has had
relations at Daneshill & Tudor Hall. The first time he came
Nidnod showed him round wearing that old blue bathing
dress which is very tight and liable to split at inconvenient
places. Lady Mayhew-Saunders came to lunch yesterday
with Anna who is very attractive and obviously pregnant.

Serena Alexander has had to go to Australia as her mother is v. poorly. We enjoyed the Derby in our posh stand and had a marvellous view. Nidnod thought Willie Whitelaw was the caterer! There were some semi-pissed youths outside the Derby Arms who exposed themselves to young birds in passing cars. As it happens there was a chilly wind and their display aroused contempt rather than excitement.

XXX

D

An absolute classic by my mother. Fortunately Willie Whitelaw (the recent Home Secretary) was too polite to comment.

Budds Farm
18 August

Dearest L,

I hope you are behaving yourself with reasonable decorum in Devonshire. I expect that in fact you are asleep most of the time, the local climate hardly being conducive to vivacity. I suppose you do very little walking or bicycling now that you drive a powerful motor-car. I went on a holiday to Devonshire – possibly Newquay – nearly seventy years ago. I remember nothing about it bar my disgust on finding a dead hen behind our bathing hut. Talking of hens, Emily is coming to Kintbury with us. The move is making progress: your mother is in her element – Order, Counter-Order, Dis-Order! I have done quite a lot of work in the garden. I was having a quiet pee on the rubbish heap when I found our daily standing one yard behind me. Too late to stop! I am showing Major Surtees the house today. He has just bought a house in Wylye (Wiltshire). Mr Parkinson is having a worrying time with all his relations and has chronic indigestion. Aunt Pam is coming to see the house on Tuesday. I can anticipate some sarcastic comments. The General has declined to come. Aunt Pam has a new dog, a King Charles Spaniel. V hot here which is an economy as I need not wear socks. Otto is well; he possesses common human failings, being greedy, randy, cowardly and sly. Perry is getting heavy and pompous. Aunt Boo was on TV yesterday; I assume on some programme dealing with mental instability. I was sorry to hear about your roof leaking. Will the insurance cough up? Insurance companies delight in evading responsibilities. I have just had a bill for nearly £9,000 from Lane-Fox and Co and that is only the start!

Love to you all from both of us,

D

Aunt Boo had been interviewed about one of her many latest obsessions, which included 'Keep us out of the Common Market' and 'Keep Dorking white'. My brother was very kind to her and was her carer for many years. He said that she was one of life's genuine nutcases. There wasn't a political party that she hadn't stood for at one time or another.

The Miller's House
Wednesday

My Dearest L,

How are you doing? Have you nudged anyone in your car yet? Yesterday I had to go to a funeral at Newmarket. Luckily Sir John Mayhew-Sanders drove me up in his Daimler. I began to chew my knuckles when we did 135 mph on the Cambridge by-pass! The car had a telephone on which my driver rang up the Russian ambassador. In the cemetery I noticed a tombstone with the rather odd name on it of J. Barrington Waterfall. Young Master Mayhew-S asked me if I was opting for burial or cremation. I replied 'Sanitary Disposal'. The previous day I drove Nidnod to Sandown for lunch with the Directors. She wore a new ginger wig, drank a lot of gin and sat next to a journalist with no hair but a beard like an acre of moss. I sat next to a v rich lady in the insurance business. I thought I got on well with her. She made, I found out, a lot of inquiries about me afterwards. She may have fancied me or she may have been collecting information to pass on to the police. The two dogs are v tiresome, peeing on every stick of furniture and biting visitors to the house. Some visitors look as if they wished there was a lethal chamber operating in Kintbury. Mrs Surtees came to lunch today and your dear mother talked a great deal of balls. Aunt Pam comes to lunch on Sunday, Aunt Joan had a good holiday in sunny Malta. Emma L-R has a steady boy-friend which annoys her mother. Did I tell you Cousin Caroline sold 6 yearlings at Newmarket and got 962,000 guineas? My bath overflowed and has damaged a ceiling, thereby rendering me unpopular.

I gave Nidnod a present for her work in moving, i.e. a side of smoked salmon, a stilton cheese, and several jars of honey. I think I saw a picture of Charlotte B in the Tatler.

Best love to you all,

D XXX

The infamous wig. We persuaded our mother to get a real hair wig at great expense. After several outings she announced that it did not do her justice and returned to her nylon wig (cost approx £30), which could go in the washing machine on a 40 degree cycle.

The Miller's House
16 November

Dearest L,

I am delighted to hear you are going to increase the population of this troubled world. I sometimes wonder what sort of world it will be in 50 years time; or whether there will be a world at all! When I was born there were far more horse-drawn vehicles in London than cars. No one had flown the Channel and middle-class families had six indoor servants, some of whom were paid less than £20 a year. Golden sovereigns were in use rather than £ notes. Happily no one could foresee two ghastly wars with the cream of the nation destroyed in the first one. Cinemas were just starting and the posh one was at Marble Arch. Life was more peaceful without wireless or TV. People died in large numbers from tuberculosis, bronchitis, appendicitis, pneumonia, diphtheria, typhoid and scarlet fever. In 1919 more people died of a virulent 'flu germ than were killed in the whole of World War I. The country began in the Edgware Road and I well remember the blacksmith's shop there. My grandmother had a large estate with a farm at Harrow which was as rural then as Kintbury is now.

We have got 24 people for lunch on Sunday and I foresee hideous chaos.

Best love to you all,

D

Doom and gloom with the world as I announce that I am pregnant again.

The Miller's House
Sunday

Dearest L,

How are things going with you? Have you flogged your house yet and found a new one? Life is fairly quiet here. I got a £10 fine for a parking offence in Newbury. I am refusing to pay so may end up in gaol. My bed is very uncomfortable so I am going to jump on it for quite a long time today to try and alter the contours. I keep losing my spectacles, car keys, house keys, cheque book, pension book and library cards; part of the gagadom inseparable from old age. I am now on the Committee of the Animal Health Trust; whether any animals will benefit from my appointment seems doubtful. Unlike most other members of the Committee, however, I do not kill animals for pleasure, though of course I eat a good few. I think tearing corpses apart with your teeth is rather disgusting and I rather wish I was a vegetarian tucking into nut cutlets and fricassée of parsnips. I wonder how many dead animals one devours in a lifetime? Quite a lot if one includes shrimps and whitebait. How awful if the animals got organised under a sheep like Scargill and started devouring humans. I must say any animal getting my liver would be dead unlucky. Only 23 shopping days till Christmas! How I look forward to the traditional Yuletide songs like the one that starts

'As she toasted him a crumpet

He tickled her under the umpet.'

Thank God we are not going away for Christmas and no one shows the faintest inclination to spend Christmas here. I expect your mother and I will share a Sainsbury's meat pie in front of the electric one-bar fire.

XXX D

'This will be my last Christmas, you will all miss me when I am gone,' my dad was frequently heard to say around this time of year.

1985

The Miller's House
12 January

Dearest L,

I hope you had a happy birthday and lots of presents. It is
horribly cold here but this house is much warmer than Budds.
Last Wednesday I had to let Otto out at 7 a.m. Unfortunately,
dressed only in pyjamas and dressing gown, I fell down on
an icy patch in front of the house and could not get up! As
Nidnod was in London, I felt I might freeze to death but after
taking my slippers off I managed, despite two more falls, to
reach the door. I had some coffee with whisky in it followed
by a hot bath and gradually recovered but I am still bruised
and shaken. How I loathe old age with all the horrible things
it inevitably brings with it! I'm very clumsy and forgetful
these days and I fear Nidnod finds me boring and irritating.
I can't really blame her. We met Dr Keeble having lunch in
the Dundas Arms with a v. plain lady (wife?) whom he did

not introduce to us. I had to buy a new loo seat – £40. The electricity bill is double what it was at Budds. The Gaselees' daughter nipped off just before a party and had her hair dyed purple. Her parents were NOT pleased! No hot water in Aunt Joan's flat and all the loos on the floor above have frozen up. A nasty three-car crash at our turning up to the house yesterday. You can get rather good whitebait at the Three Swans in Hungerford. I'll take you one day. I have bought a birthday card of quite hideous vulgarity for your sister.

Best love,

D

Moving to The Miller's House was supposed to make my parents' life easier. Unfortunately my dad was not as stable as he used to be. This incident shook him up badly and he was very lucky not to have broken something.

Budds Farm
19 January

Dearest L,

A good start to the morning: Nidnod fell on the stairs, upset a cup of coffee, injured her knee and shouted Fuck! A lot of snow here but we are still mobile, but only just. Poor Aunt Joan has no hot water and there is not a loo working in her block. No lark when you're 77. Poor Major Surtees, moving into a new house in Salisbury, has found that four crates containing all his most treasured possessions have been stolen. I hear you've bought a mansion in the fashionable SW area. Let me know something about it. I was born in SW3, 11 Cadogan Gardens, a big house but short of loos and bathrooms. From there my parents went to 49 Charles Street, W1, just off Berkeley Square, then to 40 Sloane Court, SW3, and finally, their last house before shifting to a flat, 28 Cadogan Square, SW3. I think Lord Cadogan has a flat there now. Their first flat was a very posh one at 76 Sloane St. The flat underneath was owned by a retired Ambassador, Sir Percy Loraine (Pompous Percy) who went abroad for the winter during which time his butler used the flat as a brothel. My mother could not understand the weird noises that could be heard from 2 p.m. onwards. I think my father rather enjoyed them. The Van Straubenzees came to lunch with a son of 20 who is already as bald as a billiard ball. Nidnod never takes her wig off nowadays as it keeps her head warm. Reverting to my parents' houses, they had some weird domestic servants: a butler who forged cheques and went to prison; a parlour maid called Murphy who was usually pissed and fell flat on her face at a dinner party when carrying in the soup; a butler called Ellis who helped himself from the cellar and peed in the bottles he emptied (he went to prison too); a butler who had been wounded in the head and chased the cook with a bread-knife; a very good butler who came from the Camerons but unfortunately was a roaring homo; and an admirable cook whose brother was a big noise in the CID. We also had a chauffeur who drowned himself in quite a shallow puddle.

Best love
R

P.S. My parents' old daily, called a charwoman in those days, lived in Cadogan Street where I believe houses now cost about £250,000!

When my father visited me in London we would often make a tour of the houses where he had been brought up. He had learnt to ride a bicycle in Upper Sloane Street – only a lunatic would attempt to do that now.

The Miller's House

Dearest LL,

Was it you who sent me an alluring Valentine? If so, many thanks. I've been feeling so mean and frozen, I simply lacked the heart to send any this year. I got a very saucy one from the ex-Mrs Surtees. The winter is tolerable when you're young and active but a proper bugger when you're old. Most of my exercise consists of filling coal scuttles and log baskets and cleaning grates. The Vaughans came to lunch last week; I gave them a 'Between the Sheets', 1/3rd Naval Rum, 1/3rd Cointreau, 1/3rd Spanish brandy, a squeeze of lemon. It got them talking which was one of the objectives. In the evening we went to a truly horrible party in aid of the Vine & Craven. Noisy, boring, and I have never seen so many plain individuals under one roof before. Lupin comes down here tomorrow. Has he married a dusky beauty, do you think? The Parkinsons are still pushing the boat out in Australia. The Wallis's son John runs the posh hotel in Sydney. Major Surtees enjoyed

Kenya where he saw several wart-hogs. Joy's husband has had his hip operation which was a success. I saw frogmen searching for a body in the Canal on Sunday but they did not hook out anything when I was watching. Poor Old Lord Carnarvon is now 87 and sadly a complete cabbage. He lives in Edgecombe Nursing Home. A lot of rich people crawl off there to die. I watched Crufts on TV. When I was a boy the Crufts Champion one year was poisoned by suffragettes.

Best love to you all,

D

P.S. Thanks so much for coming down yesterday and cheering me up.

Each year my dad and I would send each other the most unsuitable Valentine's Day card that we could find and sign them from totally inappropriate people, such as Myra Hindley or Bernadette Devlin.

The Miller's House
1 July

Dearest L,

How are you behaving, pretty indifferently I suppose. Nidnod has just left for Wimbledon and it has just started to rain. This evening we are due to attend some bizarre festivities in a marquee given by a local bigwig whom I hardly know. Horrid scraps of food in cardboard pastry and warm white wine bottled at Staines. I stayed at Brighton with Cousin John on Monday. He has some muscular affliction and can hardly walk, while in addition his lower intestine is giving tiresome trouble. I was nearly killed when I had (or rather my car had) a tyre burst doing 70 on the M25 in the rush hour. However I faced Demon Death with a sangfroid based on indifference. I am not good at changing wheels and the tyre was in ribbons. Two young men came to my rescue and spurned any form of reward. Ghastly party chez Carden next Monday. Tepid Pimms and fish salad! Whoopee! Joy had a good holiday in Malta but was slightly surprised to find her excellent hotel was owned by Colonel Gaddafi. Had a very nasty lunch with the Oldfields; meat you could re-sole an army boot with. Bent my false teeth quite badly. Jane sent me a poem by Piers. A second Lord Byron? On the whole I think not.

XX XX D

Demon death was always waiting round the corner for my father. Luckily (I am not quite sure how), he survived a variety of prangs. Despite my father having once been an excellent driver, his driving skills were very poor in the last years of his life.

The Miller's House
8 October

Dearest L,

I gather your Scottish holiday was a flop. I don't care for Scotland or the Scotch; take my advice: never go north of

Watford. How is that cheeky Benjamin? Thank you, I will come to the christening if I can. I ought to be at a funeral at Honiton today but I really can't drive there and back on my own. Nidnod is in poor form and keeps on grumbling about this house, Kintbury, and the locals who are mostly elderly, tedious members of the middle class, just like ourselves. Next Saturday we go to Colonel Thistlethwayte's 60th birthday party. I must try and keep sober for the drive home. Otto pinched a liver sausage at breakfast and doubtless will be horribly sick. The Burnaby-Atkins are just back from a smashing trip to China. Aunt Joan is pushing the boat out in Cyprus.

    XX D

When my parents first moved to The Miller's House my mother took an unwarranted dislike to Kintbury, mainly because she could not keep her beloved horse nearby. Sadly she did not keep this to herself and could often be heard complaining about there being too many worthy, bridge-playing octogenarians in 'effing Kuntbury', which is what she rechristened Kintbury. When the dust settled she actually made a number of good friends in the village.

The Miller's House
27 October

Dearest Lumpy,

Thank you so much for inviting me to Benjamin's christening. I think it all went off very well. Benjamin is very much in my good books as most babies take one long, hard look at me and are then sick in a slightly cynical but thoroughly offensive way. You have not told me yet what he would like for a christening present. I think I told you the very nice tall parson who took the service is a son of my former Commanding Officer, Sir John Whitaker, a huge man who smoked 80 Gold Flake per day and who died suddenly out shooting. I once had to share a room with him in Jerusalem and he snored like a Chieftain tank in bottom gear. I thought Rebecca looked very nice. What does she want for Christmas? Have you seen this month's Tatler? Who is the girl on the front cover? She looks a really saucy little number! Nidnod is in very bad form: she never stops banging on about how she hates this house and the inhabitants of Kintbury. I like it here but I suppose I shall be forced to leave.

Best love,

D

Benjamin's christening went off without a hitch or any family rows. My brother Lupin had just returned from New York and came with my parents. For some unknown reason he had dyed his hair bright orange but kept denying it.

The Miller's House
10 November

Dearest L,

I hope you are all thriving. We have ten people to lunch

today which means a lot of fatigues. I am giving them a fair whack of vodka on arrival to cheer them up. They are all about 74 years old. Your mother has been to church but I stayed behind to do the grate, fill log baskets, decant the port etc etc. It was supposed to be a short service but there were six hymns and a long sermon by a man with a beard. There was a murder down the road on Thursday, not an exciting one, just a domestic row that got out of hand. There have been two rather frightening rapes at Silchester. Your mother is in poor form and complains that the house is damp. Aunt Joan is 78 on Nov 18, I am 76 on the 22nd. There is something rather horrible about old age. I think Jane is going to send her sons to Marlborough. My father was there, also, I think one of Henry's brothers. It used to be very Spartan and the moral standard was low as so many of the boys were the sons of parsons. An extremely large cat has taken up residence in the garden here. I think he is quite capable of eating both the dogs. I have a nasty feeling that something is wrong with our drains. More expense! I had a nice two days at Brighton with Cousin John who is slightly eccentric but very rich.

Best love,

D

My father loved to escape to his cousin's luxury penthouse flat in Brighton, complete with an extremely inebriated butler. I am unsure what held the greater appeal: comfort or an extensive library of pornography.

24 November

Dearest L,

I enjoyed seeing you yesterday and I hope it was not too gruesome for you being surrounded by old fogeys. Thank you for the generous gifts which were greatly appreciated. Lupin gave me a huge picture of the Coldstream Guards charging with fixed bayonets. I'm glad I wasn't there, it looks very rough! Nidnod is the better for her trip to Scotland but is not right yet. I think she sees Dr Yates on Friday. The first sentence in a book I was given is 'old age is not really so bad when you consider the alternative'. Unless you are fed up with it I'll send you and Henry smoked salmon as usual for Christmas.

Best love, D

P.S. We had a nasty fire down the road this morning. It started in an airing cupboard. The smell of burning flesh is rather awful.

My father's seventy-sixth birthday. As yet another year passes he is full of the joys of life. It was one of the last occasions on which the whole family congregated at The Miller's House.

Gloom House
Kintbury
Friday

Dearest L,

Many thanks to all members of the Gowan Avenue mob

for their generous and tasteful Christmas presents. The pretty egg-coloured bow tie will detract attention from a pustular spot on my Adam's apple, while the desk diary will doubtless soon be crammed with reminders for scintillating social engagements (I don't think). In fact the most common entry will be 'Threatened with gaol if tax still unpaid on this date.'

I have sent Rebecca some money and I hope you and Henry will receive some fish by Dec 15th. I have not forgotten Benjamin. I will discuss the subject of a suitable gift for him when next we meet.

Nidnod is poorly today with another cold. My sister is in poor shape, having had to consult her GP for the first time for 15 years. She is very gloomy, being unused to feeling unwell. As a matter of fact being 78, on your own and seedy is pretty depressing.

Peregrine tried to eat me last night. Otto is in very good form, greedy and incontinent.

XX D

My father looks very dapper in his new bow tie, as yet unstained with egg or marmalade.

1986

The Miller's House
7 January

Dearest L,

I hope the Nidnod expedition went off well. I have sent
you off a birthday present; don't panic if it does not arrive in
time. How old are you? Getting near the dangerous thirties
I suppose? It is snowing hard here. Desmond P took one of
his mothers-in-law out to lunch just before Christmas. She is
85 and totally gaga. There was no conversation as the old girl
never stopped singing Three Blind Mice! When she gets bored
in her Home, she upsets Ovaltine over the matron's head.
Poor Desmond has another mother-in-law living with him. No
hospital or home will take her and either Desmond or his wife
has to be in the house with her. They are worn out. Aunt Joan
is not too well and at 78 is starting to feel her age.

  XX D

Poor Mr P. seems to endure a bottomless pit of impossible mothers-in-law.

The Miller's House
28 February

Dearest L,

No bricks through your windows yet, I hope. What a shaming programme! It beats me how four allegedly educated young men could voluntarily depict themselves before millions as pig-ignorant fascists with just a hint of cruelty thrown in. That individual called Cheney struck everyone here as a genuine chateau-bottled shit. He and the others must have won thousands of votes for the Labour Party and the League against Cruel Sports. There is an old saying that whom the Gods wish to destroy they first render insane.

Your mother's birthday today. Naturally after reading the papers – abuse from the Mail, contempt from The Times – she is a bit shattered. What does Lupin think of it all?

Best love,

D

My father considered himself to be a thoroughly respectable, middle-class gentleman and he would avoid any sort of publicity. To say he was horrified when Henry got involved in a documentary called The Fishing Party was an under-statement. My parents had invited several friends around to watch the airing of said documentary. It made it all the worse as they honestly thought they would be watching a programme about four prosperous city men taking a fishing holiday in Scotland, their aim being to catch the world record for skate. What emerged was the outspoken, even outrageous, point of view of four very right-wing and not very intelligent young men.

The Miller's House
15 March

Dearest L,

I hope that black dog of yours has not devoured anyone yet. We went to Sandown on Friday and I have seldom been colder. However we had a good picnic in the car – bacon sandwiches and whisky macs. The worst dressed man on the course without any doubt at all was Loopy! Your mother hunted on Saturday and did not have too bad a day. Jenny Burnaby-Atkins dropped a 12 lb frozen turkey on her foot and is not surprisingly hors de combat. She and Freddy are due to go to Morocco on the 24th. Morocco is full of male members of the English aristocracy who go there in pursuit of Arab boys. The Lemprière-Robins had a smashing time in Thailand; the hotel they were at made Claridges seem like a tramp's doss-house. I visited Major Surtees' new house in Wiltshire; it needs a woman to live there and some furniture. Our dogs are yapping more than ever and they do a fair amount of indoor peeing. Mrs Cameron is in Denmark where it is even colder than here but it is, after all, her home country.

The Danes are less boring than Norwegians and less morose than the Swedes. They produce very good pornography.
Love to all,
D

My father describing Loopy as the worst dressed man on the racecourse really is the pot calling the kettle black.

The Miller's House
20 April

Dearest L,

I hope all goes well with you. I expect London is depressingly grey and chilly. It has been a shade warmer here and the garden is crawling reluctantly to life though quite a lot of herbaceous plants are in fact dead. Your sister and her sons came for three days. Piers managed to lock himself into his room and we had to get the local Fire Brigade to release him. Piers has a lot of quiet charm but Nicholas is too much of a mother's boy at present. For God's sake don't tell Jane that or she'll get Colonel Gaddafi to bomb The Miller's House! Nidnod has a bad leg which makes her a bit crusty. The east winds play havoc with my temper and I don't suppose I'm any too easy to live with. I was going to London for a wedding (Fortescue-Ainsworth) on Thursday but now I must drive down to Sussex to go to the funeral of an old friend (Brigadier Henry Green) who mercifully died after a ghastly stroke. I have been lumbered with writing his obituary. Major

Surtees is staying near here and there are rumours that his presumed impending marriage (his 3rd) is after all unlikely to take place. Is Henry taking part in the London Marathon? I am thinking of lining up for a ½ mile sponsored walk for certified Kintbury geriatrics.

Best love to you all,

D

Only a lunatic or masochist would dare to criticize my nephews. Luckily they have both turned out to be happy and successful in their own right.

Kintbury

Dearest L,

Thank you so much for your letter and the photographs, both greatly appreciated. Benjamin looks a very cheerful character. Possibly I did at that age. In 1910 there were very few cars, about six aeroplanes that looked like bicycles with wings. The British Navy was easily the strongest in the World. I had two World Wars ahead of me, five years in prison, men walking about on the moon, the threat of the atomic holocaust, the decline of this country into third-rate power! I was brought up with seven or more indoor servants, including a butler and a footman. Now at 76 I do the grate, fill the log-baskets, clean my shoes, make my bed, cook and wash-up my breakfast, wash my car, do endless weeding fatigues in the garden, dig up huge piles of ground elder, join huge queues at the surgery. Quelle Vie de Dog! My father was wounded in World War I, my grandfather in the Indian Mutiny!

Nidnod did not enjoy the wedding and came back in a fractious mood. It was a 2 hour drive to Henry Green's funeral and it was a 2 mile walk from where we parked the car to a tiny church. Luckily a seat had been kept for me as the church was full and lots of distinguished generals could not get in and had to stand shivering amid the tombstones during the service, rather a long one as we sang all 5 verses of Onward Christian Soldiers! Brig Lemprière-Robins got stuck in the traffic and arrived when the service was over. He had cut himself shaving and there was blood all over his collar! Give my love to Big Emma; I hear Emma's father is coming to live near Marlborough.

Love to all,

D

Did you read the obituary of Henry Green I wrote for 'The Times'? I was given 15 minutes to do it.

My father contemplates his present and past life as he attends yet another good friend's funeral.

The Miller's House
Saturday

Dearest Lumpy,

How are you keeping? I imagine the delights of spring in Devonshire have been blunted by Siberian winds. East winds are very damaging to the liver and tend to make everyone unhappy and bad-tempered. How is Henry? His little trouble with the BBC was only a seven day (or less) wonder and seems to be completely forgotten. I imagine the drink trade does well this cold weather; people drink to avoid hypothermia or to try and make themselves slightly less miserable. I made myself a big cocktail last Tuesday with lots of cointreau and cognac. Unfortunately a front tooth (almost the last one) contacted a solid block of ice, and as was the case of 'The Titanic' with the iceberg the tooth came off second best, being split from bottom to top. The dentist removed the remains the next day. I can no longer say, like the lady at the Hunt Ball in the 'Irish RM', 'I have only two teeth in my head but thank God they meet!' My appearance and powers of mastication have certainly not been improved. Lupin was down here and seemed in good form. Do you think he will be the first Mortimer millionaire? It was kind of you to have Nidnod to stay. She likes seeing you and the children and she is apt to get bored and crusty here. The garden is in a ghastly state; everything looks dead and probably is. I have got to go to a wedding in London this month: I am told the bride is known in SW3 as 'Horizontal Harriet'. I am thinking of resigning from the Turf Club as I only use it twice a year. All the members I knew are dead, or just about to be, and I have nothing in common with the younger members.

Best love to you all and keep in touch,

D

Much to my mother's chagrin my father was given false

teeth that never seemed to fit him properly. Under pressure,
he would put them in for special occasions (if he could find
them). When guests overstayed their welcome he would
remove his teeth and place them on a nearby table.

The Miller's House

Dearest L,

Happy Easter to you all and I hope you have all
recovered from influenza. Yesterday Nidnod drove me to
lunch with Mrs Cameron in my car. We missed a crash (her
fault) by inches at a roundabout and when we reached our
destination she removed much of the left-handside of the
car when parking it. It will costs hundreds to put right. I
can't understand how she did it as it was before lunch, not
afterwards! I have just backed Mr Snugfit for the National;
his owner runs the Snugfit Trouser Factory. Julian Seaman
rode at Liverpool yesterday and came down at the very first
fence. Your brother seems to have become an antiquarian
bookseller: he has tried everything except running a brothel
and being a jockey. The Tordays are coming for Easter: I
am locking up anything of value which is breakable. I am
busy helping to organise a beano at the Highclere Stud in
aid of the Animal Health Trust. Unfortunately I am apt
to fall asleep during committee meetings. Our secretary is
blonde and very attractive. A very peculiar woman called
at 9.30 the other evening and said she had come to buy a
potter's wheel! I think she had escaped from the local funny

farm. We have been invited to a posh lunch at Ascot on Wednesday and Nidnod is polishing up her chestnut wig. On the other hand I am in dire need of a haircut. I have been doing odd jobs lately for 'The Field' and 'Racing Post'. I need the money. Paddy Parkinson's son Simon brought off a nice double the other day; in the morning he failed his driving test (the man who tested him was a big black man), and in the evening he was mugged, losing valuable possessions. He is retiring to Cyprus for a holiday. Willie Whitelaw was the last head boy of my preparatory school before it went bust; next in seniority was Desmond Parkinson. Willie W would have been blown up at the Conservative Conference only he was sick of politicians and went for a quiet night at John Blackwell's flat. Our first daffodils are only just coming out, but plenty of snowdrops and violets.

Love to all,
XX D

This is Lupin's favourite story about my mother's wig: He and his partner Tim were spending one of many evenings at The Miller's House after my father had died. My mother, having had quite a few too many, wobbled outside (as only my mother could wobble) with her Chihuahua, Danny. Several minutes later Danny reappeared without my mother and promptly 'killed' her wig on the sitting-room floor. On further inspection my mother was found head first in the hedge at the bottom of the garden.

The Miller's House
23 May

Dearest L,

The holiday was a success and Jane made an admirable travelling companion, good-tempered and unselfish. The journey was a smooth one, 5½ hours from door to door. At Marseilles airport we picked up a hired Peugeot which served us well. The hotel lies in beautiful country with marvellous views. The temperature was always between 75 degrees F and 80. There are only 14 beds in the hotel which was by no means full. Very comfortable and excellent service. Nidnod never stopped talking incomprehensible French and invited all the hotel staff to come to Kintbury! Luckily they realised she had a few marbles missing! We had the pool to ourselves for most of the time and even I took the plunge four times a day. The food was very much 'Provencal' which suited Nidnod and Jane but I yearned for Marks & Spencer fishcakes and Nidnod's kedgeree. The girls put on weight, I lost a bit as dinner did not tempt me. We had delicious picnics every day in wonderful country full of irises and lilacs. The one failure was when I stupidly asked the barman for a Pimms; it tasted like treacly furniture polish. The dogs were pleased to see us back and the weeds had thrived in my absence.

Without my asking for it, I was given a free copy of 'The Times' with my breakfast which I took care not to have with 'les girls'!

Best love to all,

D

Your mother's back is giving her trouble which makes her

querulous. She is judging at Windsor Park for two days. Your brother is here and seems in goodish form. He tells me you are being given a posh new motor.

After years of loyal service my bright green Renault 5 succumbs to rust problems and the engine literally falls out in the middle of the King's Road. Lupin, rather surprisingly, finds me a great second-hand red Golf, which even more surprisingly is in very good nick.

The Miller's House
7 June

Dearest L,

I hope you are reasonably well. Luckily it has not been very hot which presumably would not suit you. Has that black dog of yours managed to survive the London traffic? At enormous expense we have had all our carpets cleaned as they were all stained beige by dog pee. We went to the Derby and had a marvellous view from the Directors Box. We had a good picnic in the car-park first. We have had a lot of lunch parties lately, all pretty boring on the whole and some rather peculiar things to eat. We went to a funeral on Monday (Lady Fisher aged 89). A short service followed by tea and cucumber sandwiches in the garden. Tomorrow we motor to Somerset for lunch with Fitzroy Fletcher. On Wednesday there is a beano at Highclere in aid of the Animal Health Trust. I have met Steve Cauthen quite often. He is intelligent and well-mannered. He stays at Brighton with Cousin John. Your mother is no nuttier than usual and is mad on gardening. We are just off to eat smoked prawns at The Harrow at Great Bedwyn. I have just had a very vulgar post-card from Emma L-R. I am sending one to her that will make her hair stand on end (I hope). Freddy Burnaby-Atkins came to lunch and I mixed a drink that made him pour with sweat. I'm afraid this letter is hideously dull but I feel liverish and senile.

Best love,
RM

Much to my father's bewilderment, he and my mother continued a busy social life, about which he would write to us, normally including dubious encounters and hilarious anecdotes about the other guests.

5 August

Dearest L,

Thank you so much for kindly inviting me to your country estate. I think you are making it very nice. It only needs a little flowing water. Geriatric visitors don't really fancy peeing out of the window at 3 a.m. We had a smooth drive home except when Nidnod annoyed a lady driver who called her some fancy names.

Love to the children.
Your loving father,
D

We are struggling with no running water, a regular occurrence living on a farm but not ideal with my parents staying. Although I had put buckets of water by the loo to use when flushing, I caught my dad peeing out of the window.

The Miller's House
8 November

Dearest L,

I hope you are well and behaving with reasonable decorum. Your mother is suffering a lot from insomnia; I can sympathise, as for two months after my accident I seldom dropped off to sleep before 3 a.m. I shall be 77 on the 22nd. I find old age fairly revolting but at any rate it does not go on forever. I feel very fragile nowadays but at least I can still see and hear. I am having trouble with my left knee and the therapist who has been working on it has not been noticeably affective. Do you watch EastEnders? The son of an old friend of mine has just married the attractive Indian girl who works in a shop. His parents are not exactly overjoyed. Joy moves house next month to Thatcham. I can't believe she will work here much longer and she will be a sad loss to your mother. Cousin John is in hospital at Oxford for a spinal operation; he seems to be going on all right. His sister Mary has been staying here plus two Norwich terrier bitches who have caused our dogs to pee all over the place. I dread Christmas which makes me wish I was a Jew or a Hindu. One of my godsons has retired to a Trappist monastery and seems content there. I rather think his mother is becoming a Buddhist! Aunt Pam is pretty groggy and not strong enough to go and see her horse run at Windsor today. Saucy Piers asked me 'What goes in dry, comes out wet and gives two people pleasure?' Answer: A tea-bag.

Love to all,
D

My father manages to escape with his life after a head-on crash with a lorry on a country lane.

The Miller's House
30 December

My Dearest L,

Thank you so much for the book you so kindly gave me and which I shall greatly enjoy. I am most grateful. Christmas went off pretty well chez Torday. Jane worked like a slave and produced some excellent food and I am very keen on her turkey porridge. Paul was extremely generous with the drink and I consumed a great deal of champagne. Piers has a lot of charm and is very easy to get on with. Nidnod fell for Giles Milburn, aged 5. He is certainly a dear little boy. All the Milburn children have exemplary manners. We had drinks with an affable man called Bates; his wife has done a bunk. We drove home in pouring rain. On the M6 the roof rack on the car in front collapsed and 6 suit cases were precipitated on to the road. We just managed to avoid them. I did not envy the unfortunate individual who had to collect his belongings in teeming rain and in face of holiday traffic. Nidnod hates this house and wants to move. I suggest she waits till I cool which won't be all that long the way things are going. I think we shall all go broke in 1988 so keep your larder well stocked!

Happy New Year (I hope) and best wishes to Henry, Rebecca and Benjamin,

XX D

The affable man (aka Tommy Bates) turned out to be my sister's 'new male friend'. He is now her husband and is a delightful, intelligent man of whom we have all become very fond.

1987

The Miller's House
Sunday

Dearest L,

I hope you are keeping well and are not too tired. V cold here and a fair amount of snow. Nidnod has been poorly with a sort of virus, bad catarrh and sore eyes. Alas, I am not all that hot in the role of Nurse Dillwater. Cheltenham went off OK except that it got progressively colder. I did not see Loopy but spotted him at Sandown for the Grand Military. I think I was slightly better dressed than he was which is not saying much. The crowds at Cheltenham were gigantic. Luckily Nidnod is quite unscrupulous over parking and got us a pitch in a handy place reserved for geriatric members of the Jockey Club! We only had to walk 25 yards instead of about 2 miles. James Pope is not exactly noted for his brain but his daughter has got a scholarship to St Mary's, Calne. We had a very good dinner with total strangers called Sidebottom. Mrs S had quite a big moustache. We had a hilarious lunch with Tony and Rosie Villiers who are both nut-cases and pay periodic visits to a funny farm. Mrs Pope has an excellent cook and the browsing and sluicing were superb. The dogs are well but lead a most irregular sex life. A very tiresome woman called yesterday; I had to tell hideous lies to get rid of her. I go to London next week for a Derby lunch given by the sponsors. I anticipate indifferent food and acute tedium. Major Surtees has a new girl friend, a bit boring but a good figure. Aunt Pam is back; there is no truth in the rumour that she had a walk out with a big, blond Life Guard who had pulled her out of the surf at Bondi Beach! No news of Lupin. I believe Jane is looking in here soon. I am cutting some boughs of holly so that I can flog the boys if they get too noisy.

Love to all,

D

My favourite story about my father-in-law, Loopy. Back in 1969, after a Rolling Stones concert in Hyde Park, Lupin and Pete Carew (his best friend and Henry's brother), then sixteen, were arrested outside a nearby telephone box. Loopy and Lady K happened to be passing and, seeing the boys being hustled into a police car, were in a state of shock. Loopy's immediate reaction was to follow the police car. When Loopy and Lady K caught up with them at the police station, they discovered my brother had a small amount of marijuana in his pocket. Loopy immediately put it in his pipe and tried to smoke the evidence. He was lucky not to have been arrested himself.

The Miller's House
23 June

Dearest L,

How are you behaving? Nidnod is exhausted after an afternoon of riding with the disabled. Tough work for a woman of her age! Stuart, the boy she is in charge of, is quite a comic and gets a real kick out of it. Ascot was fun and the weather was marvellous. Nidnod backed the winner of the Hunt Cup at 20/1. Of course Ascot is no longer smart like it used to be; the aristocracy has opted out of racing which has no more social significance than dog-racing at Catford or Slough. Most of the women are dowdy and appear to have escaped from the annual garden party of a Rural Dean at Okehampton. Not many young girls to be seen. Some familiar faces among the men, including one old buffer, the stains on whose waistcoat are real turtle when he is betting successfully. Very cold and dank the last few days; we went round a marvellous garden yesterday kept by a man who plans draining systems all over the world. Wheatcroft, the great rose man, lost 65,000 roses at his nursery during the winter. I went berserk in Marlborough today and bought a lot of clothes, including some moccasins which I now find are 2 sizes too small. They might fit you! I tried to buy a red shirt but could not find the right size, perhaps fortunately. I bought a jersey for Nidnod, dark blue with white hearts on it. She likes it. I also bought some rubber mats to place under wash basins, a new design which can be trimmed to fit with nail scissors. I hope Rebecca did well in her ballet class. I shall expect her to dance 'The Dying Swan' next time

I see her. I am having a new sort of kedgeree tonight, bright yellow and rather smelly. Baron Otto is in excellent form and hasn't bitten many people recently. I watched the local Morris Dancers yesterday. Their first number was 'The Old Man's a Bag Full of Bones'. This was followed by 'Gathering Peasticks'. I longed to join in.

Love to all,

D

Lupin comes here on Wed., the day our dining room table comes up for sale.

The dance of the dying swan from Swan Lake was one of my dad's party pieces. His performance involved a lot of energy and rather less dignity, and would have us all in hysterical laughter.

The Miller's House
26 June

Dearest L,

V hot and sweaty here. I am just off to Salisbury with Gordon Richards to judge two year olds. Champagne lunch with Sylvia Bowditch. Nidnod is flying to Jersey for Emma's dance. Alas, thunderstorms are forecast. Lunched yesterday with the Bomers. Mark has taken a very good degree at Cambridge. William is teaching in Martinique. Your brother is looking for a larger flat. Three Marlborough boys have been sacked for 'vandalism', smashing up a swimming pool and some science schools. I met a parson at Ascot who told me his nephew had been at Marlborough, taken up drugs and had been in and out of prison ever since. My father hated Marlborough which was hideously spartan in his day. Piers has taken up bell-ringing. Mr Randall was a bell-ringer in Salisbury Cathedral. He told me that a fellow-ringer was only 4ft tall and had to stand on a box. One day the rope got entangled in the little man's foot and he was hauled upside down to the roof! The Lloyd Webbers have bought all Sydmonton from Clifford Kingsmill who is now an alcoholic. We sold the dining room table for £1,800 and have bought a smaller one. I bought 2 rather nice water-colours for my bedroom. I have sold my leg in Easdale for £425; I'm sorry for the girl who bought him for 'eventing'. We had a picnic on the Downs last night; Nidnod forgot the soup and the corkscrew.

Love to all,

D

Despite the fact my mother forgot the corkscrew, I can guarantee that she managed to open the bottle in one way or another.

The Miller's House
24 August

Dearest L,

Black skies and thunder, a fitting end to a fairly hideous summer. Lupin and his bird lunched here yesterday, I like her very much. Pity she has a husband. My cheerful local taxi driver was killed in the massacre; his wife has just had a baby. Luckily we were in the 'Galloping Crayfish' while the carnage was going on outside. I quite enjoyed Jersey; most of it resembles the suburbs of Bournemouth and so do the locals. I would not care to live there; Guernsey, I'm told, is worse. Nidnod is not too well but battles on gamely. I feel my age which is nearly 78. Old age is full of little surprises, most of them of a fairly hideous nature. Most of us are doomed to end up in the Hotel Incontinental! I hope Benjamin has got over the pox; it is a good thing to have it young. Your poor mother suffered grievously when she had it when she was over thirty. We are off to lunch with Derek Colls today. He seems to have defeated cancer of the throat; his wife died of that awful disease. Freddy Burnaby-Atkins is in the Isle of Skye with his younger brother who has Parkinson's Disease, another victim of which is Emma's father. Charlie Blackwell has sold 1,000 bottles of vintage port left by his father and has had his house completely done up. Lupin is staying with Cousin John at Brighton tonight.

Love to all,

D XX

Having heard the news and knowing my parents were in Hungerford on the day of the massacre, I had tried to ring them several times without luck. When my mother finally answered the phone she was extremely irritated and could not understand what the fuss was about. They had been lunching in the back room at the Galloping Crayfish and were more concerned as to how they were going to get home to feed the dogs than the threat of being shot by a madman.

The Miller's House
Sunday

Dearest L,

Only 87 shopping days till Christmas (or something like that)! I rather dread the winter although the summer is usually pretty dreary too. Nidnod and I thought of having a party to mark our 40th wedding anniversary but we have given up the idea as we cannot think of any form of celebration that would be amusing and would not involve inviting bores. Possibly I may have a lunch party in London but that is improbable. Perhaps I shall go off and get quietly pissed on my own! I had a night down at Brighton with Cousin John last week. His flat is super-luxurious and I had a marvellous view of the marina from my bed. The Brighton shops (including the fish market) are good and the streets are full of retired actors doing their shopping accompanied by their boy-friend. Nidnod is none too well and I am rather worried about her. She gets terribly depressed and her lack of energy is very untypical of her. Jane's godfather Peter Black has had a nasty heart attack but is recovering. He is very depressed at having to have his tiny dog, about half Otto's size, put down. The weather here is awful, grey, chilly and never a break in the clouds. Freddy Burnaby-Atkins is just off to Turkey and I rather envy him. You ought to persuade Henry to take you there. Hungerford is recovering from the massacre; they had not had a murder there since 1870 when 2 policemen were shot by burglars. There is supposed to be a memorial to the policemen but no one seems to know where it is. I hope Piers is settling down at Eton. The day before he left he was heard discussing on the telephone with a friend which Bank he intended to patronise. I hear Rebecca is becoming very horsey. Well, if it was not ponies it would probably be boys! Joy is on holiday and so is Mr Randall. I think Mr Randall is having a spree at Weymouth. Major Surtees is just back from Turkey where he had a marvellous time, no doubt in the harems. His grandson (or one of them, at any rate) goes to Eton this term. He shows promise as a poet.

Love to all,

XX D

The Randalls (my parents' faithful gardener and his lovely wife) certainly made the most of their increasing years and spent more and more time on coach trips.

24 October

Dearest L,

Thank you so much for your letter. Yes, our holiday was a fiasco due almost entirely to bad weather. The villa was very comfortable, had a marvellous view, a charming garden and a lovely pool but the rain teemed down continuously. The local tavernas were repulsive, and revolting food was served grudgingly by dark, hairy women who looked like Welsh rugby forwards. The Robins had bad colds, Nidnod 'flu and I weighed in with diarrhoea. Coming home we drove like demons in heavy rain to get to Faro airport in time only to see a notice posted saying that owing to crew shortage our flight was delayed by six hours! Luckily we had not handed in our rickety hired car, so went on a tour and after a lot of sticky drinks in peculiar bars found a seaside grill where a huge man dished out the best fried sole I have ever eaten. We arrived at loathsome Gatwick 9 hours late but luckily our hired car (Mr Robey of Highclere) was waiting for us (his bill for the 2 journeys was £100 and it was money well spent) and we reached home knackered to the tenth degree at 10 p.m.

We got off lightly in the storm. One wall down (£1,200 to repair), a big shrub uprooted and various tiles dislodged. Lambourn got away with it completely. We only lost electricity for 12 hours whereas the Parkinsons were without power for 5 days. The poor Robins had a terrible time in Jersey and had no electricity or water for over a week. The drive was blocked by fallen trees and they could only reach the road by driving over fields. They lost over 100 trees and their lovely woodland garden has literally ceased to exist. My friend Tom Egerton had an avenue of 120 chestnuts, every single one blown down. Lavinia Norfolk was found in tears surveying the damage at Arundel. St Peter's, Eaton Square, where I went to the children's services over 70 years ago, has been destroyed by fire, and Chester Square is in a fearful mess with fallen trees.

I first met Lester P when he was a boy of 15 staying for Brighton races at the Royal Crescent Hotel by himself. He was lonely and I used to drive him to the races, and if it was fine we sat on the beach or even bathed in the morning. Owing to his speech and hearing difficulties, conversation was not easy. He told me about his life at home and said that to keep his weight down he got very sparse meals. He complained of being undernourished and said that whenever he caught a cold he came out in running sores. The sad thing is he never got any fun for his money.

Nidnod is cubbing today. I hope that old horse does not die on her. It's about your age! I'm sorry for your friends with kidney stones. I've had them and I'm told it's as bad as having a baby. Sorry Rebecca is idle; I do sympathise with anyone who takes life easy at school. I was always unwilling to exert myself.

Best love,

D

My father had a soft spot for Lester Piggott and was visibly upset when he was convicted of tax evasion and jailed for three years. In the end he served 366 days.

The Miller's House
Sunday

Dearest L,

How are you all? The season of runny noses and racking coughs is just beginning! I was hoping for a quiet morning here but Otto has had diarrhoea and has been sick over my bed. Thanks very much! On Wednesday I dined out with Mrs Surtees at West Ilsley. I got home soon after ten, intending to enter the house by the electrically operated garage door. However, on pressing the appropriate button nothing happened. I had locked up carefully before I went out and there was no alternative way in. Realising I was for a night in the open unless I extracted my finger, I drove to Hungerford Police Station and explained my little predicament. The police were most helpful and two young constables returned home with me, guaranteeing to get me in somehow. They failed to force a window in the sitting room but eventually, by means of a jemmy, forced open the window of the downstairs loo. Luckily the burglar alarm was not working. Nor were the lights, and once I had remembered where the switch-box was (in the gent's loo) it was found that the trip switch was non-operational and thus the garage door was not working, nor anything else operated by electricity. I eventually crawled into bed, very weary, long after midnight. The next day I had a puncture in Kintbury but luckily found a man keen to change the wheel. Your mother is due back today and I think has enjoyed her visit to Jane. I couldn't find much I wanted in the kitchen and have been living on stewed apples and grape-nuts. Desmond Parkinson had a birthday party on Friday and provided an excellent lunch. Otto came in for a bit and was not worse than fairly objectionable. I have bought two new pairs of spectacles in Hungerford but don't see very much better. I saw Aunt Pam yesterday looking rather haggard. She had come to lunch here the previous Sunday and there was a deathly hush when Lady Carden said 'I suppose you are Cynthia's younger sister'! Nidnod was wearing a new chestnut wig that looked like a broody Rhode Island Red. Lupin was here, looking seedy and complaining about his leg. I do wish he had better luck with his health. Aunt Joan wrote to complain that her friends have developed a tiresome habit of dropping down very dead indeed.

Love to all,

X D

My father's life still seems full of adventure. Having reached the age of seventy-eight he would rather have opted for an easier life.

The Miller's House
19 November

Dearest L,

Thank you very much for your saucy card which I greatly enjoyed. Nidnod drove me to London and we gave Aunt Joan a birthday lunch at the Turf Club where the chef must have been having an 'off' day. The trifle was like a mauve cowpat. Aunt Joan is pretty good for 80 and has never needed a pair of spectacles. I look forward to seeing you on Nov 27. I have ordered an uncomplicated lunch in the hope that the chef cannot make a cock of it. I had a Christmas card today from Basil Madjoucoff, as usually a very holy one. I am tempted to send him a cutting from Playboy. I am in for a merry afternoon, having some false teeth fitted (at hideous expense). I expect after a fortnight I'll give them to the Boy Scouts Jumble Sale (White Elephant Stall).

Best love,
D

Basil Madjoucoff was my father's interpreter during his time in Palestine before the Second World War. He never failed to send my father a Christmas card, including all his news, every year for some sixty years.

1988

The Miller's House
20 March

Dearest Lumpy,

I enjoyed seeing you last Sunday. Come again soon. I'm sorry you are having rather a worrying time due to the recession and the general financial situation. I've been through the mill myself. I worked for the 'Sunday Times' for 28 years and during that period it changed hands twice, each time for the worse as regards individuals such as myself. I never knew if I was going to be taken on by the new lot. I have worked for 'Raceform' since 1946 and more than once they have tottered on the brink of insolvency. I shall never get a golden handshake when the time comes for parting as apart from them being hard up, they are very mean indeed! I once got a job on the 'Sunday Times' for a man who was a bit pushed for Lsd; once he was settled in, he tried desperately to secure my job. Thanks awfully! His son got 12 months inside for stealing books from his College Library at Cambridge. If things get a bit sticky at your end, don't hesitate to call on your parents for help. We can probably dig into our jeans for a few quid even if it means flogging a couple of pictures or some Scott silver. Items like school fees are so desperately expensive nowadays. I think when I went to Eton it was something like £80 per term and a suit of grey flannels was £5. I enjoyed my lunch in London on Monday. I don't often sit down with a Bishop. I remember the Bishop of Lincoln as a young officer with the MC. He was in the running for Canterbury. Also there was the Regius Professor of Modern History at Oxford. He had a good war record. The Duke of Devonshire said he remembered the bad language I had used to him when he was a cadet in the Eton OTC. I sat next to Lord Sinclair, a truly delightful person I had last seen in hospital in Edinburgh in 1945. Brig Robin was there and we both regretted we were too old to go and see an improper film afterwards.

Love,

D

Nidnod had a blow-out at the Berkeley with her old boy friend Rodney Carrott.

Despite my father moaning about a lack of treacle, if there was a specific problem he would always dip his hand into his pocket and magic up some lolly.

The Miller's House
23 March

Dearest L,

Thank you for your letter. I'm delighted to hear the children are flourishing. Your mother is hunting with the Vine and Craven today but it is very wet and there is talk of cancelling the meet. Brig. Lemprière-Robin is staying here but has a fearful cold. I'm glad I didn't go to Cheltenham; I believe it was hell, especially on the Thursday. The poor old Queen Mother was forcibly embraced by an inebriated butcher from Roscommon. Democratic days! My few remaining teeth are all falling out and I can hardly bite into a blancmange. We had a very good lunch on Sunday with Miss Pope and Nidnod made sheep's eyes at an old major from the 17th/21st Lancers. We looked at the hospital Nidnod is going to. It appears clean from the outside which is something. It is not a very pleasant operation but she is facing up to it with her usual pluck. I went to a big lunch at the Hyde Park Hotel and sat next to a very agreeable MP (Labour) who is member for a Newcastle constituency. He is nuts on golf and thinks Willie Whitelaw is marvellous. Cousin John is very lame with a poisoned bunion.

Best love to you all,
D

Just over a year after my father's death, the family gathered for 'The Roger Mortimer Memorial National Hunt Novices Race' at Sandown; one of his favourite racecourses. My mother and Lupin were invited to join the Queen Mother for lunch in her private box. Towards the end of lunch, the Queen Mother and the other guests' attention was drawn towards the balcony where my mother was jumping up and down, shrieking in support for jockey Gardie Grissell (a family friend) who was neck and neck on his way to winning the Memorial race. Unfortunately my mother's wig flew off her head. Unabashed she picked it up, placed in back on her head and carried on as though nothing had happened. Rather generously the Queen Mother and Lupin agreed between them that as this was my father's race, my mother should be allowed her moment. I am told the other guests in the box looked on in horror.

The Miller's House
28 September

Dearest L,

How are things going with you? I'm pleased to hear that Henry has had a bit of luck. One needs that in life more than anything. It has not been exactly hilarious here: Nidnod has got fearful depression which does not make her exactly easy. I dare say I'm both exacting and annoying, a really irritating type of old man. I haven't been all that well and at times my favourite reading has been catalogues from cremation companies, including 'Special Offer' services. I don't fancy a recorded service with prayers by the Rev. B. R. Morgan-Jones. The moment the coffin starts sliding out of view can be trying for anyone at all fond of the corpse. At that moment in the cremation of an unpopular bookmaker one of his Clerks was heard to whisper to another Clerk, 'For Gawds sake don't press Button B, we might get the Guv'nor back.' A bookmaker's family was returning home from the old man's funeral. En route his son said to the sorrowing widow, 'Mummy, Daddy did die of diarrhoea, didn't he?' 'No dear,' the widow replied, 'not diarrhoea, gonorrhoea. Daddy was a sportsman, not a shit.' I don't think that's a very nice story and I ought not to have related it to a pure and innocent girl like you. Piers and Nicholas are staying here for two nights and I hope they'll cheer Nidnod up. Lupin seems quite happy and his work with that Pimlico antique firm keeps him busy. Uncle Ken was knocked over by a woman backing her car yesterday. Shaken, but not seriously hurt! John Surtees paid an unexpected call here. He is now 72, has shed two wives, but looks young and healthy. I fear he has lost quite a wad of money in the Lloyds affair and has had to give up his London flat. Luckily an ex-girl friend has invited him to use hers when he needs to. Offer accepted! I have known John for 51 years, including 5 years in prison. We saw a lot of each other after the war before I took Nidnod to the altar and we had some very good times which I have no intention of letting you know about. Anna was my first god-daughter; I'm afraid her husband is seriously ill. The Parkinsons are in Paris for a week. I first went to Paris in 1928 when I was just 18. The exchange was very much in our favour and I had a marvellous time on very little money. Here again my lips must remain sealed! The Burnaby-Atkins have just left on a 3 weeks safari in Kenya. I have had no adventures in the Far or Middle East but I went fishing off Suez in 1937 with a very nice Italian who made lavatory seats. I came under fire for the first time in my life in Jerusalem in 1938 when a cross-eyed Arab had a pot at me when I was inspecting a Jewish school. With slightly better eye-sight I think he would have got me. It was in Palestine I had to see an Arab hanged before breakfast. He had committed a rather nasty murder but I felt sick. I liked Palestine; I had Christmas in Bethlehem, Easter in Jerusalem, but the one place I liked was the Garden of Gethsemane maintained by German monks.

I was on parade in Hyde Park in 1936 when some tipsy Irishman tried to shoot the King but missed with ease. It was about that time that I was on Bank of England Guard and before I left at 6.30 a.m. I filled in a form saying nothing unusual had happened during my tour of duty. Unfortunately there had been a rather bad burglary but no one had bothered to wake me up. I got into a little mild trouble. I took part in two Aldershot Tattoos; the first one I was a Roman soldier taking on Queen Boadicea; the second time it was a drill display with no words of command given. At one of those performances a charger trod on his groom's foot and the groom's comment 'Get off my fucking foot' re-echoed around the arena as unfortunately the groom was standing just by the microphone.

I have been asked to review a book entitled 'Prep School' but found it terribly dull and refused. The chapter on sex was a great disappointment and the boys interviewed were desperately unenterprising.

Your affectionate father,
RM

Lupin has started working for the infamous Hobbs brothers at their new antiques showroom in Pimlico.

The Miller's House

Dearest L,

Many thanks for a birthday card (slightly late) and a Christmas card (somewhat early). Both appreciated, though. I had a lot of birthday cards, mostly connected with sex. Freddy B.A. sent me a group of plump, naked German girls getting up to larks. I left it in the bathroom where it was found by your mother! My sister sent me a vulgar book on sex for geriatrics and the Parkinson one on how to run a brothel coupled with some instructions which rather surprised me.

Best love,
D

1989

The Miller's House
18 January

My Dearest L,

I'm so sorry I was not back in time from my stroll on Bedwyn Common to say good-bye to you and Henry and the children. I had not realised you were going back to the 'Smoke' before tea. It was very good of you to come down here and help Nidnod and apart from that I very much enjoy seeing you, a somewhat rare pleasure I'm sorry to say. I thought Rebecca and Benjamin both behaved remarkably well; of course Rebecca is growing up fast and I expect a certain amount of decorum from her: I was not disappointed in that respect. Make the most of the children when they are still with you; you really don't see much of them once they are at boarding school. I used to love the seaside holidays when we were all together. I think I am very lucky in my grandchildren but I expect sooner or later they'll give you a few worries; they would be unnatural if they didn't.

Alas, my watch stopped this morning and it was 8 a.m. when I let the dogs out. Very unpopular!

Love to you all,

D

For years we would spend our summer holiday in Brittany, always staying in the same hotel, a great favourite which was on the beach.

The Miller's House
3 April

Dearest L,

Marvellous spring weather. I've just taken Otto for a stroll on the Downs. We had a lot of people in for drinks yesterday including 2 8-month old twins! Quite a jolly man with young wife who runs the Newbury Arts Festival. Someone who shall be nameless did in a bottle of vodka! Drinks before lunch with the Parkinsons; slept hoggishly afterwards. I gave Nidnod a charming card featuring a jaundiced-looking hen and an outsize egg. I watched the Boat Race on TV (can't think why). Some of the Oxford crew are as old as me. The B-Atkins are off to Austria. Since Freddy joined a Lloyds syndicate they are up to their tonsils in treacle. I've just had a jumbo-sized bill for water and sewerage! We are having 2 nights in dreary old Devonshire in May, followed by 2 days in sleepy Somerset.

Love to all,

D

I always enjoyed going on walks with my father. When I was young he would make up stories about 'Jowler the Giant'. As I grew older he started to regale me with anecdotes about his years as a POW, which he would always make amusing.

The Miller's House
Friday

Dearest L,

I enjoyed seeing you the other day. I'm sorry Henry can't come on the 26th but these things happen and collecting a small party is never easy. Have a good time in the West Indies and mind out for black men on dark nights! Peregrine is all the better for his trip to Devonshire and I hope it did Nidnod good too. I left my spectacles behind. I saw the specialist in the R Berks Hospital today. She was v pleased with my progress and I don't go again for a month, which is good news.

Love,
D

My father arranged a small gathering at the Turf Club for his birthday. He took great of pleasure in introducing me to his racing friends, some of whom looked as though they had not long left for this world.

The Miller's House
8 August

Dearest L,

Had an excellent lunch with the Popes today: really good stewed plums and cream. Emma L-R called in for a drink with her young man of whom I formed a goodish opinion. Dr Yates goes on holiday today: he is tasting wine and food in Burgundy. Lupin has left for Zambia. Piers is doing something to underprivileged boys in Dorney, just outside Eton. Nidnod bought Chinese prawns for supper last night from a caravan in Kintbury. Reckon I was lucky not to get salmonella. At the Popes I met a funny little man called James Holford whom I first met at Wixenford in 1919. His parents removed him in 1921, fearing his morals were being corrupted (by no means improbable). At Eton he coxed the eight. He went into the 15/19th Hussars: Loopy may have known him. If I can get seats in October, will you come to Show Boat with me? I saw it at Drury Lane in 1928!

Love to all,
D

Show Boat was a huge success. My father got into the spirit, tapping away to the songs. I think I even saw a little moistness around his eyes.

The Miller's House
9 September

Dearest Lumpy,

Thank you so much for having us to stay. You are certainly making your house very comfortable and attractive. As for Rebecca and Benjamin, they are everything that grandchildren should be – or hopes they will be. Sorry the picnic aborted. Having eventually found our way from you, the joke is that Nidnod thought she was in Lynmouth the whole time she was circling ghastly Ilfracombe. We went to Lynmouth on Sat: Nidnod bought herself a bath-mat and me a jumbo ice cream and a key ring with my name on it! Good strawberries for dinner on Sat: also roast duck. We got home today in 2 hours dead. This evening we go to a golden wedding beano with hymns and speeches! I shall love that! Poor Nidnod is suffering from depression and needs a holiday.

Love to all,

D

Have a good time in Norway. Take warm undies.

I actually managed to have my parents stay in Devon without incident.

1990

The Miller's House
Saturday

Dearest L,

V. pleased to see you looking bronzed and well after your holiday. Benjamin is good fun and looks happy.

The day of Pam's funeral a letter arrived to Pam from a Senior General. In it he expressed his sympathy with Pam over Ken's death. I know Generals are apt to be thick but this takes the professed bun with almost insolent ease.

Nidnod went cubbing today but came home early as she felt awful (and looked it, too). I twisted my knee putting my trousers on today and am as lame as a geriatric camel. I can't go to Ascot in consequence. I found a spider as big as a mole in my bath this morning. Luckily Jane did not find it or she'd have had a fit! I hope you had a jolly evening at Slough, less posh than Ascot I suppose. My horse is called 'Owners Vision' (why?). It is a big common brute that could pull a brewer's dray. Do you know the difference between a war-horse and a dray horse? The former darts into the fray, the latter farts into the dray.

XX D

Having no children, my aunt and uncle were devoted to each other. Uncle Ken was Aunt Pam's carer for a number of years and was completely devastated when my aunt passed away.

28 February

Dearest L,

How are things going with you? I hope you have not had a lot of tiles blown off! It has been very stormy here but we have had so far only one power-cut. My type-writer is kaput so now I have no car and no writing machine. Combined with my ill health and Nidnod's tantrums, life is not exactly a bowl of cherries. The Gunns came to dinner on Saturday. Diana is a real nut-case, albeit a charming one. She has an ever-loving husband; both drink neat whisky. Diana's mother is 96, totally gaga and it is a full-time job looking after her. Nidnod is only 69 and I suppose easy by comparison but she finds me more or less impossible and I find her looking at me as if nothing would give her greater pleasure than to hear I had been squashed flat by a no. 19 bus or perhaps a no. 22 on Sloane Street. The new Kintbury District Nurse is Portuguese and rather attractive. While I was waiting my turn in Surgery last Monday a man had a heart attack. We are lunching with the Watkins today and to Nidnod's horror are scheduled to watch racing films afterwards. I hear Lupin's blood is in a somewhat unsatisfactory condition. George Wiggan is very ill with hepatitis in Africa and his wife and daughter have flown out to see him. On Friday I lunch with Burnaby-Atkins. He and Jenny are just off on a Pan-Am special offer trip to Mexico which includes a free car for a week and several days free in a post hotel.

I think all the people I know in this area (including myself) who are thoroughly depressed should line up and take a running jump in the River Kennett, having first filled their pockets with large stones. I did hear something about Lady de Mauley but I've forgotten what. Peter Walwyn lads' hostel was burnt down the other night but luckily no lives were lost. Mrs Grace Walker lunched here on Sunday. She is 86 lives alone and is the nicest and most intelligent woman in Kintbury. Dr Yates is off to Paris, his motto is 'Most diseases are incurable my job is to try and make them more bearable'.

XX D

Love to all

My father is truly lost without his good old-fashioned manual typewriter. Under pressure, he bought a Japanese electric typewriter which was not a great success and soon taken back to the shop. Incapable of ever getting the upper hand in any commercial transaction, he part-exchanged his new, hardly used, electric typewriter for a second- or third-hand manual typewriter. He could not have been happier.

1991

Dearest Lumpy,

Thanks for your pretty card. I'm glad you enjoy working for the Conservatives. I fear you'll be out of a job by the next election. Very damp and cold here. We go to London on Thursday: I rather dread it. Your mother has fibrositis and wants to go to Baden Baden for a cure. She is off to Jersey for a week in July if she can find a keeper for me. I'm not looking forward to Ascot, I'm too old for that sort of lark. I enjoyed seeing Rebecca the other day and liked her shy friend from Dorking with out-of-door teeth. All my dahlias have expired.

Best love, D

Much to everyone's surprise I have got a job working for the Conservative agent for Kensington & Chelsea. As my qualifications are minimal I am happy just to stuff and stick envelopes. My father took to calling me at the Conservative office every day. He had a soft spot for Charlotte Blacker,

who had given me the job, and I think he was hopeful she
might answer the phone and cheer up his day.

Dearest L,

What ghastly times we live in! The Gulf, The IRA, terrorism, unemployment, ghastly weather! I don't seem to have had much peace since that day in 1916 when I was doing French with Miss Shaw my rather pongy governess when a lot of aeroplanes flew over Cadogan Gardens. We only discovered later they were German. Years later during a dock strike I was marching guardsman down to Smithfield when an elderly striker shouted 'You wouldn't shoot your fellow workers would you?' and my platoon Sergeant shouted back 'Yes I would Grandad and in the balls!' My mother, of all people, worked in a canteen during the general strike and was generally acknowledged the Queen washer up! She washed up – it was the job she liked above all – in two major wars and various big strikes. When I was about 10 Field Marshal Sir Henry Wilson was shot by Irishmen on his doorstep quite near to where we lived. The murderers were caught and hanged. There was a particularly sordid murder about the same time in the house where Aunt Boo lives now. Uncle Tony, my mother's brother and my god-father, was a splendid character, the larky mobbing type. He was arrested on his 21st birthday party for breaking up a Masonic dinner at the Café Royal and careering down Regent St waving the master mason's insignia. He hated the war, got an MC, was badly wounded and was killed when his ambulance was hit by a shell. He gave me a gorgeous tiger skin when he came back from India, my mother pinched it for an evening coat but I got it back in the end. My father went off to Le Torquet for a beano and in his absence Ellis the butler drank up all the hock in the cellar, peeing in bottles after he had emptied them. At about that time we had a parlour maid called Kate Murphy who was pissed at a dinner party and passed out carrying a tureen of turtle soup. Another butler attacked Mrs Tanner the cook with a carving knife and another one, who had come from the Camerons, tried to have the footman.

XX D

In the final year of my father's life things went downhill quite quickly. It was really hard for the whole family. Sadly this is the last letter I received from him. As is often the case he became very clear about the early years of his life but would forget what had happened that morning.

This little ditty would always make me laugh when my father recited it:

Poor old banana stood up in bed.
Along came sausage and bopped him on the head.
Poor old banana fell down dead.
Tripe and bananas brown bread.

Acknowledgements

Thanks to my brother Charlie, aka Lupin, who has been the driving force behind *Dear Lumpy* . . . as well as being a constant throughout the trials and tribulations in my life; Tim (Partington), my brother's partner and my best friend who has provided endless emotional support; finally to Victoria Young who is the angel in my life.